Joseph Gallifet

Devotion to the Blessed Virgin : its excellence, and how to practice it

Joseph Gallifet

Devotion to the Blessed Virgin : its excellence, and how to practice it

ISBN/EAN: 9783337305055

Hergestellt in Europa, USA, Kanada, Australien, Japan

Cover: Foto ©Lupo / pixelio.de

Weitere Bücher finden Sie auf **www.hansebooks.com**

DEVOTION

TO

THE BLESSED VIRGIN.

ITS EXCELLENCE, AND HOW TO PRACTISE IT.

BY

LE PÈRE DE GALLIFET.

Translated from the French.

LONDON: BURNS AND OATES.
1880.

TRANSLATOR'S NOTE.

The first part only of Père de Gallifet's work is here translated.

The second, which is nearly the same length, forms a collection of original prayers to the Blessed Virgin.

TO THE BLESSED VIRGIN

MOTHER OF GOD.

Loaded with thy favours, most powerful Queen, from my earliest youth, nothing should be dearer to my heart than to procure thy glory, after that of thy Divine Son.

During the whole course of my life, thou, O Mary, hast continually fostered in my heart this just and holy desire.

It still remains with me in the extreme old age to which I have now arrived, and in obedience to its promptings I have composed in thy honour this little work. I lay it at thy feet, O Queen, beseeching thee to take it under thy protection, and to command thy angels to shield it from the attacks of the devil.

For my own part, my dear Mother, I die content, in leaving behind me this slight token of the respect I feel for thee, of the love I bear thee, and of my gratitude for all thy mercies; and if it should contribute in any way to the increase of the devotion which is thy due, I shall be more than satisfied.

Devotion to the Blessed Virgin.

CHAPTER I.

IN WHAT CONSISTS DEVOTION TO THE BLESSED VIRGIN.

There are three acts, or principal sentiments, which constitute the essential part of devotion to the Blessed Virgin. These are:—

First. A sentiment of respect, veneration, homage and submission suitable to her dignity as Mother of God.

Second. A sentiment of confidence, proportionate to her power and goodness, which induces us to have recourse to her in all our wants, as to our helper and our refuge.

Third. A sentiment of tender and filial love, excited by her perfections, her motherly care of us, her great goodness, and the benefits by which she surrounds us.

These may be termed essential, and hence infallibly arise all the other affections by which devotion to the Blessed Virgin ought to be perfected.

The three sentiments of respect, confidence, and love, constitute, then, the essence of such devotion; so much so, that every feeling which does not spring from them, or tend in their direction, should be regarded as altogether extraneous.

Any one who is wanting in these sentiments will certainly be wanting in devotion to Mary.

On the other hand, whoever possesses them will be filled with admiration of her greatness, and with affection, confidence, and love in her regard. With an ardent desire to consecrate himself to her service, and to become worthy of her protection, even the most culpable sinner need not despair of his conversion, through the intercession of such a holy Advocate.

I may here be told that I am omitting one of the principal features of devotion to Mary, viz.—imitation of her virtues. Is not that the test after all? Without that, can there be any true devotion to the Blessed Virgin?

Attend to my answer—it is essential to the subject.

Imitation of her virtues is, doubtless, the best ornament of devotion to Mary, but is, at the same time, its fruit rather than its essence. If devotion to her consisted in the imitation of her virtues wherever the latter were not practised, the former could never exist; whence it follows that only just and holy souls could pretend to such devotion; all sinners would be excluded.

God forbid that we should approve a sentiment so contrary to the teaching of the Church, which calls Mary the hope and the refuge of sinners, and which invites them all to have recourse to her with the greatest confidence.

It is certain that a sinner may be devout to Mary, without imitating her virtues.

The essence, then, of this devotion, must be sought in those sentiments common both to the just and to sinners.

A sinner, in the same way as a just man, may be touched with feelings of love, respect, and confidence, with regard to this merciful Advocate.

Experience forbids us to doubt that such dispositions are very real in many sinners, who, in consequence, practise many exercises in honour of the Blessed Virgin.

They keep her feasts, enter confraternities dedicated to her, and perform the duties which these impose; they fast, and give alms in her honour; they visit her churches, and frequently invoke her name.

All this indicates, no doubt, real devotion to Our Lady, and upon it the following reflection should be made.

Like all other virtues, devotion to Mary has different degrees; without attaining complete perfection it is, nevertheless, possible to practise it to an inferior extent.

When very perfect, it produces imitation of the virtues of the Blessed Virgin, and renders those who practise it more conformable to her, and more agreeable in her eyes, thus causing them more and more to deserve her patronage and protection.

The same devotion, however, may be as yet so feeble and imperfect as not to produce this fruit of *imitation.*

Such is the case with many sinners; but, all imperfect though it be, it exists, it has a place in their hearts, and is a germ of life which God allows to be there.

If cultivated, it in the end produces the fruit of true repentance, and of a perfect conversion.

It is of infinite consequence to the salvation of such poor sinners, that they should not stifle in their hearts, or root out this germ of life; and yet unenlightened zeal, ignoring the merit of any other, would make all devotion to Mary consist in the practice of her virtues.

What would be the result of this doctrine, and of declamations against such as believe they have devotion to the Blessed Virgin, though they continue to live in sin?

When they are told that theirs is a false devotion, which is even injurious to the Mother of God, who encourages neither impenitence nor the enemies of her Son; that it is only hypocrisy on their parts, and a vain and criminal confidence—what, I ask, is the result?

It produces this sad and deplorable effect—it causes the sinner to abandon the holy practices he had begun in order to do honour to the Blessed Virgin, and to merit her protection; it weakens the love he had for her, and causes him to lose the confidence he ought to feel in her compassion.

A wise and enlightened zeal acts very differently.

When it finds in the sinner any sentiments of devotion to Mary, it neglects no opportunity of fostering this seed of grace ; it cherishes it, and assists its growth, for it well knows, by constant experience, that devotion to this compassionate Mother, and all practices of piety which have reference to her, are, even in the greatest sinners, gifts of grace, by which God disposes them to obtain, one day, by her intercession, their complete conversion.

By how many examples might this be confirmed! how many sinners are there, who, having preserved in the midst of an evil life a certain devotion to Mary, and who, feeling their hearts touched by love for her, have prayed to her, invoked her name, and exercised holy practices in her honour, have found therein a source of salvation!

Pious books and the annals of the Church are full of such instances.

In speaking of devotion to the Blessed Virgin, let us then bear in mind these three essential characteristics; let us employ all our eloquence and all our power, in order to excite these three sentiments; and when everything has been said that is capable of inflaming the hearts of those who listen, take care lest the work should be spoilt by unseasonable declamations which only serve to weaken their good intentions.

They should take their leave, on the contrary, full of admiration for this glorious Virgin, full of wonder at her goodness, her mercy, and the power of her intercession; full, in a word, of veneration, confidence, gratitude, and love.

What sinner does not know that he cannot hope for salvation without renouncing sin and doing penance?

There are, however, different ways by which to arrive at this.

Devotion to the Blessed Virgin is one of the most powerful means by which to obtain from God this precious gift, and should be chiefly insisted on.

A wise and discreet zeal might, notwithstanding, remark that devotees may be found presumptuous enough to abuse what is so universally said in honour of the Blessed Virgin, as to the part she plays in the salvation of such sinners as have recourse to her.

In cases of this sort, great care should be taken that what is said in condemnation of their presumption has no deterring influence on the exercises of devotion towards her, and that it does not inspire contempt, and lead to their being altogether abandoned, as of no avail to one in a state of sin.

Continuance in these holy practices should, on the contrary, be recommended as a true means of conversion.

Following these maxims, which, according to my belief, are conformable to those of the saints, and to the spirit of the Church, I propose to speak of that true devotion to the Blessed Virgin, the nature of which I have just explained.

Let us demonstrate its excellence by explaining the three acts which constitute its true character, viz., respect, confidence, and love.

I will show how perfectly just and excellent they are, and point out the extent to which they ought to be carried by all who profess devotion to the Blessed Virgin.

Mary, after God, is worthy of all our respect, all our confidence, all our love.

Devotion to her will exist in proportion as these sentiments are lively and perfect.

Let us begin by the respect to which she is entitled, for it is the foundation of all devotion to her.

CHAPTER II.

ON THE RESPECT DUE TO THE BLESSED VIRGIN.

The respect due to any person must be proportionate to his dignity, position, and greatness.

In order, then, to understand what respect is due to the Blessed Virgin, it is necessary to consider her dignity, which is founded on her being the Mother of God.

We must pause, therefore, before this Divine Maternity, so that we may give ourselves an idea of what its greatness really is.

Let us for a few moments meditate in silence on this sublime subject.

In the first place, bring before your mind the Divine Majesty, that immense and infinite Being in whose sight angels and men, the whole world, and a million other worlds besides, more perfect than this, are less than nothing.

Having grasped the idea of this infinite greatness, look upon Mary!

She is the Mother of this great God—truly and really His Mother! To her God, in the person of Jesus Christ, she is able to say with truth and with all a mother's right, "Thou art my Son, formed of my flesh and blood. It was I who gave Thee life, and brought Thee to the light of day." Think of her as a Virgin who has received over her God that authority inseparable from the position of Mother, who beholds her God become in a manner dependent on her in becoming her Son. "And He was subject to them."[1]

In virtue of that position she enters, with regard to her God, on all the rights that a mother possesses over her son.

Think of her as a Virgin who has deserved, as far as any creature can, to enter into a union with her God, so intimate as that between a Mother and the Son she

[1] Et erat subditus illis (Luc. 2. 51).

bears in her womb, forming, so to speak, only one Being with Him.

A Virgin who was found worthy to bear within her for nine months her God, to nourish Him with her milk, to fondle Him in her arms, to clasp Him to her breast, and to caress Him as a tender mother caresses in the cradle her only child.

A Virgin whom God, in choosing her for His Mother, obliged Himself to regard and to treat as such; that is to say, to entertain towards her all the sentiments o a devoted Son, to honour, to respect, and to love her; dare we say—to obey and serve her? and who has merited the obedience and service of her God.

A Virgin who, by her divine maternity, entered into an actual alliance of the closest possible description (almost as close as the hypostatic union) with the Three Divine Persons of the Adorable Trinity, and was so intimately united to Them, that nothing approaches, or ever can approach nearer to God; who, in becoming the Mother of the

other worlds besides, more perfect than this, are less than nothing.

Having grasped the idea of this infinite greatness, look upon Mary!

She is the Mother of this great God— truly and really His Mother! To her God, in the person of Jesus Christ, she is able to say with truth and with all a mother's right, " Thou art my Son, formed of my flesh and blood. It was I who gave Thee life, and brought Thee to the light of day." Think of her as a Virgin who has received over her God that authority inseparable from the position of Mother, who beholds her God become in a manner dependent on her in becoming her Son. "And He was subject to them."[1]

In virtue of that position she enters, with regard to her God, on all the rights that a mother possesses over her son.

Think of her as a Virgin who has deserved, as far as any creature can, to enter into a union with her God, so intimate as that between a Mother and the Son she

[1] Et erat subditus illis (Luc. 2. 51).

bears in her womb, forming, so to speak, only one Being with Him.

A Virgin who was found worthy to bear within her for nine months her God, to nourish Him with her milk, to fondle Him in her arms, to clasp Him to her breast, and to caress Him as a tender mother caresses in the cradle her only child.

A Virgin whom God, in choosing her for His Mother, obliged Himself to regard and to treat as such; that is to say, to entertain towards her all the sentiments o a devoted Son, to honour, to respect, and to love her; dare we say—to obey and serve her? and who has merited the obedience and service of her God.

A Virgin who, by her divine maternity, entered into an actual alliance of the closest possible description (almost as close as the hypostatic union) with the Three Divine Persons of the Adorable Trinity, and was so intimately united to Them, that nothing approaches, or ever can approach nearer to God; who, in becoming the Mother of the

14 DEV

her hono
salvation

Pious
Church a

In spe
Virgin,
three ess
ploy all
in order
and whe
is capabl
who liste
be spoil
which o
intentio

They
contrary.
Virgin,
her mer
cession
confiden

What
cannot b
ing sin

But why should I inquire of *men* if they understand all this! Do you yourselves understand it, ye angels of heaven, ye principalities and powers, ye dominations, and cherubim and seraphim? you whose glory consists in being the servants of the living God, and who in His presence look upon yourselves, with truth and justice, as mere nothings?

Do you understand the dignity and glory of this Virgin to whom the Infinite God applies the title of Mother? who calls God Himself, her Son!

Without disrespect to the brightness of your intellects, I venture to assert that you understand it not, any more than we do ourselves.

"Let every creature be silent and tremble," must we here cry with St. Peter Damian, "hardly venturing to raise the eyes towards the immensity of so great a dignity."[1]

[1] Taceat et Contremiscat omnis creatura, et vix audeat aspicere ad tantæ dignitatis immensitatem. Dam. Serm., 1 de Nat Mariæ).

same only Son, begotten of the Eternal Father from all eternity, divides with Him, in a certain sense (to explain myself in a manner sufficiently guarded), His divine fecundity; who, in becoming the actual Mother of the Son, naturally enters into possession of all His riches; and who, at the same time, in that sublime manner belonging to her alone, is constituted the Spouse of the Holy Ghost.

You who read these things—have you ever well considered them? have you ever fathomed them? have you ever taken note of them? have you ever understood them? or are you not, at this simple exposition of them, struck with astonishment at the consideration of the elevation and dignity to which the Blessed Virgin is raised?

Do you comprehend the immensity of her glory, and understand what graces and perfections this position of hers implies? What holiness, what riches, what supernatural gifts, what privileges must accompany such infinite dignity!

But why should I inquire of *men* if they understand all this! Do you yourselves understand it, ye angels of heaven, ye principalities and powers, ye dominations, and cherubim, and seraphim? you whose glory consists in being the servants of the living God, and who in His presence look upon yourselves, with truth and justice, as mere nothings?

Do *you* understand the dignity and glory of this Virgin to whom the Infinite God applies the title of Mother? who calls God Himself, her Son!

Without disrespect to the brightness of your intellects, I venture to assert that you understand it not, any more than we do ourselves.

"Let every creature be silent and tremble," must we here cry with St. Peter Damian, "hardly venturing to raise the eyes towards the immensity of so great a dignity."[1]

[1] Taceat et Contremiscat omnis creatura, et vix audeat aspicere ad tantæ dignitatis immensitatem.

"Let every creature be silent, and remain in silence: Let every creature tremble with respect, and let none dare gaze upon the immensity of such glory as this."

"Mary," says St. Bonaventure, "is the most worthy Mother of God; even God Himself could form none more worthy. He might indeed fashion a more perfect world, a brighter heaven, but He Himself is unable to create a Mother more ennobled than the Mother of a God."[1]

"Mary," adds St. Peter Damian, "is a work so perfect, as to be surpassed by nothing but by God Himself."[2]

"In whatsoever relates to the glory of Mary," cries St. Bernard, "my devotion forbids me to remain silent, and my mind

---

[1] Mater Domini mater dignissima, ipsa qua majorem Deus facere non possit; majorem mundum posset facere Deus, majus cœlum posset facere Deus, majorem matrem quam Matrem Dei non potest facere (St. Bonav. in Speculo, lectione 5).

[2] Opus quod solus ossifex supergreditur. (St. Pet. Dam. de Nat.)

can discover nothing to say which is worthy of her; for what language, were it even that of the angels, could worthily celebrate the praises of the Virgin Mother of God?"[1]

I understand how it is that the Church herself confesses her inability to praise Mary as she deserves, and that "no praises which she is able to sing, are worthy of her;"[2] and when I reflect that there are Christians to be found, who fear they may be carried too far by what can be said of the greatness and privileges of the Blessed Virgin, I fail to understand how such a fear can arise in the hearts of any who acknowledge her to be the Mother of God.

Can any grace or privilege be for a moment compared to this? Name a single

[1] De ejus gloria nec silere devotio patitur, nec dignum aliquid Concipere Cogitatio. . . . Quæ jam poterit lingua, etiamsi angelica sit, dignis extollere laudibus virginem matrem? (St. Bernard Serm. 4 de Assumpt.)

[2] Quibus te laudibus efferam nescio.

one which does not fall immeasurably below it.

Alas! how little can any one have meditated, who is able to fear that human weakness can, by any possibility, form too high an estimate of such dignity as this.

Let us not grow weary of considering so lofty a subject.

In the particular reflections on which I am about to enter, assist me, O Lord, to impress on the hearts and minds of all who read my words, a true notion of the dignity of Thy Divine Mother, and all the respect which it demands.

CHAPTER III.

ON THE RESPECT DUE TO THE BLESSED VIRGIN (*continued*).

THAT which has been insisted on in the foregoing chapter, is only a prelude to what remains to be said on the subject of the Divine Maternity, and of the respect demanded thereby from every creature.

This quality in the Blessed Virgin may be considered in two different ways; with regard to all other creatures, and with regard to God Himself.

With regard to the rest of creatures, it raises Mary infinitely above them all, thereby rendering her worthy of a homage far greater than is due to any other.

With regard to God, it causes her to enter into a sublime alliance with the Three Divine Persons—an alliance demanding almost infinite perfection; so that in this sense the Blessed Virgin is worthy of almost infinite respect.

Let us explain these two considerations. With regard to the rest of creatures, the prerogative of Mother of God establishes Mary as queen of the universe, mistress of heaven and earth, and the sovereign of angels and of men.

"Mary," says St. John Damascene, "becomes the mistress of all creation, in becoming the Mother of the Creator."[1]

These are the titles most frequently accorded her by the Church, "Queen of the World," "Queen of Heaven," "Queen of Angels."

Here, at once, the Blessed Virgin is raised far above all other creatures; as far above them as it is fitting a queen should be raised above her subjects.

This, however, is but little: the pre-

---

[1] Maria rerum omnium Domina affecta est, cum Creatoris mater exstitit (St. Joan Damasc, lib. 4, de fide).

rogative of Mother of God, raises Mary, not only above all that *has been* created, but even above all that *could be* created.

Almighty God could give being to an infinity of creatures more excellent than those He has been pleased to call into existence; but, however glorious their perfections might render them, it cannot be doubted that they would still owe homage and submission to the Mother of their Creator; it being a matter of course, that the inferior in dignity should show respect to one of superior rank.

It is then beyond dispute that the highest dignity which even God Himself can confer on a creature, is that of being Mother of God.

Again, none of God's creatures could ever rise above the rank of servant and slave, and as St. John Damascene remarks, " Should there not be a difference almost infinite, between the Mother of God and His slaves?"[1]

---

[1] Matris Dei et servorum Dei infinitum est

Behold Mary, then, in a position where she can have no rival; where, from the very necessity of the case, she sees beneath her, all that is, or has been, or ever can be, possible to the power of God.

If you would form an idea of her glory, pause not to compare her with any other created being.

Raise your mind, at the outset, above all the saints, and angels, and powers of heaven; pause, if you will, for a moment, to contemplate the highest of the Seraphim, but only to consider that this most excellent work of the hands of the Almighty, this creature of such surpassing perfection, is himself one of the servants of Mary, who is his queen and his mistress, and that with her, in consequence, he cannot even be compared.

But let us return to the principle whence emanates this greatness of Mary — The Divine Maternity — so as once

discrimen (St. Joan Damasc. de Dormit Mar. Serm.)

more to consider this sublime prerogative.

As yet we have hardly begun to fathom this impenetrable abyss; by what remains to be said, we shall be able to gain a fuller knowledge of its profundity.

In speaking of the splendid alliance which Mary has contracted with the Three Persons of the Holy Trinity, let us endeavour to understand what great perfection it demands.

Approach the subject with all the attention of which it is deserving.

Consider that the Eternal Father, in choosing Mary to be the Mother of His Son—that the Son in selecting her for His Mother, and that the Holy Ghost in choosing her, in so wonderful and exceptional a manner, to become His Spouse, were constrained, as a necessary consequence, to render her worthy of their choice, worthy of the Divine Alliance to which they raised her, and furthermore, to heap upon her all the gifts, graces, and privileges which befit such infinite dignity.

This, though beyond dispute, remain at the same time a transcendent mystery, and is, as will be understood, the proper point from which to form an opinion concerning the dignity of the Blessed Virgin.

Consider, then, in the first place, that the Eternal Father has raised Mary to such a pinnacle of greatness, as to desire that she should become the Mother of His Word; so that this, His only Son, begotten of Him from all eternity, His equal in power and majesty, the object of His infinite love, is also the only Son of Mary, formed of her very substance; as much her Son, regarded as a man, as He is the Son of His Eternal Father, with regard to His Godhead; in virtue of which He is consubstantial with the Father. In predestining her to be the Mother of His Son, Almighty God was at the same time constrained to bestow upon her the most abundant perfections.

Can any one ask why this was ?

It was in order to render her fit to be the Mother of the Word, and to form that incomprehensible union to which she was admitted with the Eternal Father.

It was but fitting that the Divine Maternity should be upheld by the communication of perfections as infinite as it was possible for Mary to receive; and as, in the Eternal Father, His Paternity is essentially connected with all the attributes of the Divinity, her maternity should, in Mary, be connected in like proportion with these adorable perfections. The Eternal Father owed this much to the glory of His Son. He also owed it to His own glory.

To His Son,—for it was fitting that a Mother should be prepared worthy of such a Son—and how much do these words contain—a Mother worthy of the Eternal Word!

To Himself, for it was only right that He should be associated with one worthy of being the Mother of the identical

Son of whom He was the Father. These are the beautiful thoughts of St. Bernard.[1]

We can therefore say, without any fear of deceiving ourselves, that Almighty God, in raising the Blessed Virgin to the Divine Maternity, has formed the most perfect image, after Jesus Christ, of His Divinity, and the fullest and most admirable expression of His Divine perfections.

Here, then, is the first certain standard by which we may judge of the greatness of Mary—her alliance with the Eternal Father.

It was of necessity that she should be made worthy of this alliance, of being the Mother of God, and of the sublime union she had contracted with the Father.

Consider, in the second place, with regard to the Eternal Word, that he chose Mary for His Mother; that by this choice,

---

[1] Ipsa est Virginis gloria singularis, et excellens prærogativa Mariæ, quod filium unum eumdemque cum Deo Patre meruit habere communem. (St.

and in making Himself her Son, He obliges Himself to entertain towards her the sentiments of a son, and to love, honour, and benefit her in every way in which such a son ought to benefit his mother.

What a source of perfections is here!

The honour and love, due from a son to his mother, must be in proportion to his state and condition, his dignity, his wealth, and his power.

A king who allowed his mother to remain in the same position as other women would doubtless be wanting in the love and honour he owed her.

This, amongst all people, is the voice of nature, that a mother ought to be made a participator in all the possessions of her son.

It is a law engraven in the hearts of men, that a worthy son should possess nothing which his tender love does not cause him to share with his mother.

On this principle, the Son of God should endow His Mother with possessions worthy of Himself; possessions proportionate to His rank, dignity, wealth, and infinite majesty. He should share with her all His goods, and communicate to her the abundance of His gifts, as far as she is capable of receiving them.

It remains to be shown in what manner Jesus has fulfilled this duty towards Mary, and to remark how plentifully He has poured upon her all the wealth, power, glory, and majesty of which He is possessed.

I here enter upon a consideration, which in relation to the Blessed Virgin, is one of the most glorious that can be imagined, and is consequently most acceptable to all hearts that love her.

Let us not fear to give some scope to a subject so worthy of admiration, so full of delight for angels and for men.

Herein we shall experience the truth of the beautiful words, or rather of the sublime eulogy, which St. Bernard offered to Mary when he said, "Jesus Christ resembled

Mary most intimately, for all His substance was derived from hers."[1]

Remark, to begin with, the close and inseparable union which, by the will of God, exists, at all times and places, and wherever Mary and her Son are brought into juxtaposition.

Examination of the sacred texts shows that whatever the Holy Spirit has declared concerning the Word and Eternal Wisdom, *that* the Church has applied to Mary.

In the same way, if I go back to a period before the world was created, I find that Mary was united to her Son in the eternal decrees of Providence; in common with her Son, she was "in all His works the first object which God had in view." God possessed her from the beginning of "His ways." From all eternity she was predestined—"When the foundations of the world were established, and the order which

---

[1] Christus Mariæ simillimus fuit, quia totus de substantia matris genitus. (S. Bernard, Serm. 2 de Nom. Mar.)

reigns throughout, she entered into every design of the Creator, and was present in all His plans."[1]

Let us admire the spirit of the Church, which applies to Mary all the expressions made use of by Divine Wisdom in relation to Jesus Christ.

In so doing she seems to have been guided by the inspirations of the Holy Spirit.

What does she desire to teach us in thus using for the portrait of the Mother the same colours and characteristics as are employed by the Holy Spirit for that of the Son?

It is in order to insist upon the wonderful union and likeness which it has pleased God should exist between Jesus Christ and Mary His Mother.

Descending now from eternity to time,

[1] Prodivi primogenita ante omnem creaturam : Dominus possedit me in initio viarum suarum. Ab æterno ordinata sum. Quando præparabat cœlos, aderam ; cum eo eram cuncta componens. (Sap. 8.)

I find from the beginning of the world, this same relationship; whether in the promises made to the patriarchs, or in the oracles of the prophets, or in the figures and symbols of the ancient law.

In almost every one of these, Mary, equally with her Son, is promised, prophesied, and prefigured.

The first figure of Jesus was Adam—of Mary, Eve.

All the illustrious men in the old law were figures of Jesus; all the illustrious women represented Mary.

A thousand mysterious symbols have been made use of to represent Jesus; thousands of others, according to the interpretation of all the Fathers, have been types of Mary.

But let us consider this likeness existing between Jesus and Mary apart from types and figures, and according to the realities which are a part of the new law.

Here, indeed, we find it most strikingly apparent.

Let us place before ourselves the mysteries of the life, death, and resurrection of our Blessed Lord, and in them behold the intimate union which connects Mother and Son.

In the Incarnation, the Eternal Word enclosed in the Virgin's womb, and making together with her, in a certain sense, but one Being,—during His divine infancy clasped in her arms, nourished at her breast, deriving from her His support, drawing in fact His substance from hers,— in His hidden life, passing thirty years in the same house with His Mother, living at the same table, performing the same exercises, animated by the same sentiments, sharing the like fortunes —in His apostolic life, in His period of suffering, and in His life of glory, Mary is constantly at His side, participating throughout in His labours, His sufferings, and His joys.

Let us now see how Jesus bestows upon His Mother the abundance of His riches, desiring, as He does, that she should resemble Him in all He has—in His perfections, His virtues, His prerogatives, His privileges, His power, and His glory.

Nothing enhances the splendour of Mary like this resemblance: dwell upon the thought; for it is sweet, and full of consolation.

Resemblance in His perfections!

Picture to yourself on the one hand, Jesus, possessing in infinite abundance all the qualities of goodness, wisdom, power, and mercy; and on the other, Mary, ornamented by her Son with the self-same perfections which she possesses in a degree of excellence far above that which is attainable by angels or by men. Jesus is, by essence, goodness itself; that is to say, in Him are assembled all divine and uncreated perfections.

It was His sweet will, that Mary should participate in them all, and He accordingly united in her all created perfections, to an extent which raises her far above the rest of creatures, who all seem to disappear in the presence of one who enjoys the dignity of being Mother of God.

Jesus is wisdom itself, and He has filled Mary therewith to such an extent, that the Church has good reason for invoking her as the "Seat of Wisdom."

Jesus is the Father of Mercy, and Mary has well deserved to be called "Mother of Mercy."

Jesus is possessed of infinite power—Mary may be said to have the same as her Son, who renders her all-powerful.

Such are the expressions of certain of the Fathers, who place Mary in the position of queen and dispenser of all His graces and treasures.

In the purest, most perfect, most heroic, and most amiable virtues, of humility, gentleness, patience, and charity, the resemblance is still to be traced.

Jesus, of all men, possesses these and all other virtues, to their fullest extent; so, by His divine will, does Mary, of all women.

Notice again, the resemblance which

runs through their several titles of honour, and rejoice to find how the Church attributes to Mary the same qualities which distinguish Jesus.

Jesus our King—Mary our Queen.

Jesus our Master—Mary our Mistress.

Jesus our Father—Mary our Mother.

Jesus our Mediator—Mary our Advocate.

Jesus our Hope, our Refuge, our Consolation, and our Life—Mary, the hope, the refuge, the consolation, and the life of sinners.

Jesus the Path by which we must approach heaven— Mary the "Gate of heaven," the mystical ladder, by which to attain thereto.

Jesus our Guide and our Light—Mary the star which enlightens our way, which guides and directs us to the haven of salvation.

Jesus the Author of Grace—Mary the "Mother of Grace."

Jesus resembling the sun in the profusion of dazzling lights of which He is the source—Mary like unto the moon, in the soft beauty of the rays which stream down from her upon the Church.

There is a further resemblance to be found in their privileges.

Jesus, from His very nature, without sin—Mary, exempted from sin by grace.

Jesus, by divine right, free from all stain of sin, original or actual—Mary, by a special and unique privilege enjoying the same exemption.

Jesus a Virgin—Mary a Virgin.

Jesus incorruptible in the tomb—Mary also incorruptible.

Jesus rising again the third day—Mary rising after the same period.

Jesus ascending, body and soul, into heaven—Mary doing the same.

Jesus seated on the right hand of the Father—Mary placed beside her Son.

There is a still further resemblance in the power, the riches, and the glory, they each possess.

Jesus the Master of all good gifts, the Author of all graces, the King of the universe, the Lord of heaven and earth— Mary, the Mistress of the world, the Queen of angels and of men, the dispenser of all graces.

All power has been given by the Father to the Son, and all power, though dependent on Him, has been conferred by the Son on His Mother.

Every knee in heaven, on earth, and in hell, bows down before Jesus — before Mary, the knees of angels, of men, and of the evil spirits are also bent.

Finally, there is resemblance in the honours received by Jesus in the Church, and those which He desires to share with His Divine Mother.

It was His will that her name should be proclaimed, along with His, throughout the whole universe; that wherever He is adored, she should be revered; that no temple should be erected in His honour without its containing some special monument in honour of His Mother; that, together with Him, she should be an object of tenderest affection to all His servants; that the name of Mary should be inseparable from His own on the lips, and in the hearts, of the faithful; that in the Divine Office, the praises of Mary should daily be sung in unison with His own; that all the mysteries relating to His Mother, from her Immaculate Conception to her Assumption into heaven, should be celebrated as are His own; and, indeed, that feasts similar to those held in honour of the Son, should be established in honour of the Mother.

The Passion of Jesus—the Passion of Mary;

The Holy Name of Jesus—the Name of Mary;

The Glories of Jesus—the Glories of Mary; and the same of the others.

It was His will that He should, in general, be presented to the eyes of the faithful in the arms of His Blessed

Mother, and that she should be represented as above the seraphim.

This adorable Son has forgotten and omitted nothing which could make the resemblance between Himself and His Mother more fully apparent, or which could more conclusively show His determination to admit her into the participation of all His treasures.

By all these features of resemblance we see how fully Jesus has acquitted Himself of the natural obligation to which we alluded, *viz.*, that of a son towards his mother; and we are therefore able to construct for ourselves a second stand-point, whence we may form an estimate of the dignity of the Blessed Virgin.

In order to do this, we must consider the grandeur of her Son, Who chooses to share with His Mother all of which He is possessed.

To obtain, therefore, a just idea of the perfections of the Mother of God—of her power, her goodness, her mercy, her merits, her riches, her privileges, and her glory, we must contemplate her Son, and regulate the expressions we employ, and the sentiments we entertain in her regard, by those we should consider suitable in His; feeling certain that she possesses by grace and participation, as far as it is possible for any creature to do so, all that naturally, and of His own right, belongs to her Son.

We will close this consideration by a very beautiful idea, found in a homily which is attributed to St. Augustine. It treats of the glory of Jesus, and contains the foundation of all the Blessed Virgin's privileges.

The author of this homily—the third on the subject of the Assumption of the Blessed Virgin—speaking of the incorruption of her holy body in the tomb, makes use of this beautiful expression—

"If this privilege is not suitable to Mary, it is, at any rate, suitable to the Son whom she brought forth."[1]

[1] Si Mariæ non congruit; congruit Filio

How devoutly is it to be wished, that those who are so fearful of giving too much praise to the Blessed Virgin, would meditate attentively on this sentence.

As before remarked, it contains the whole principle of the greatness of Mary, and the solution of every doubt or difficulty that may arise thereupon. Her conception was immaculate; this privilege was not suitable to Mary considered merely in herself, but was certainly suitable to the Son she brought into the world.

It was not suitable to Mary herself that she should enjoy the privileges of ascending body and soul into heaven, or of being at the same time Mother and Virgin; it was however most suitable to her Son, most suitable to her, as the Mother of the Creator. The same answer may be given to whatever can be considered extraordinary in the Blessed Virgin, and if in anything we have said, or have still to say, we may be considered to go too far, we will only reply in these words of the holy doctor—

"If this appears to you unsuitable to Mary, it is at any rate no more than is due to the Mother of the Son to whom she gave birth."

As long as you persist in looking upon Mary with the same eyes as you regard the other saints, so long will you consider the praises bestowed upon her excessive; so long will you be tempted to say—"They are not suitable in her case."

If, however, you contemplate her Son, and look upon her as the Mother of the Creator; you will not fail to understand that all we say, or are able to say, falls far short of that which is her due.

Thus have thought the saints; and it is on the above principles that many of them have attributed to Mary qualities such as might appear at first sight to belong to Jesus alone; that they have, as it were, confounded the power, the virtues, and the glory of the Mother with similar qualities in the Son, as if they were not one and the same.

The Church herself seems to have adopted these views in bestowing on Mary, as we have seen, the same titles and prerogatives she gives to the Son.

To conclude.—In raising Mary in so sublime a manner to the dignity of His Spouse, the Holy Ghost was constrained to render her worthy of such an alliance, by endowing her with such eminent sanctity as might fit her to consort with Sanctity Itself.

It was but right that He should place her over His possessions, and allow her to share them with Him to the fullest extent of her capacity.

I represent to myself some powerful king who chooses for his wife the daughter of a subject; from the very moment of her becoming queen she shares the throne with her husband, she becomes a partaker in all his honours, his titles, his prerogatives, and his wealth; whatever belongs to the king, is also hers.

This example explains to us what happened to Mary when the Holy Ghost chose her for His Spouse.

St. Bernard does not hesitate to say that "at the moment when the Holy Ghost descended on Mary she received an increase and abundance of grace to the fullest extent that any creature not joined to God in unity of person is capable of receiving it."[1]

On this is founded the belief common in the Church, that Mary is the dispenser of graces, and that through her hands the Holy Ghost delights to scatter them abroad. It is in this position of Spouse that she shares with the Holy Ghost the name of Comforter, invoked as she is throughout the Church by the title of "Comforter of the afflicted;" as also by those of "Mother of Divine grace," and "Mother of Mercy."

After such considerations, founded on

---

[1] In ista Spiritus sancti obumbratione tantam largitatem et copiam Spiritus sancti accepit, quantum potest creatura viatrix recipere non divinitati unita unitate personæ. (S. Bern., Serm. de Nom. Mar.)

the Divine Maternity, concerning the dignity and grandeur of the Blessed Virgin, it would be superfluous to add more, for any others would fall short of these.

Would to God that truths so sublime, so calculated to make us comprehend what our ideas on the subject of the greatness of Mary ought to be, might flow from an eloquent pen, and be entrusted to the keeping of one of the brightest angels in heaven.

Only the tongue of a seraph is capable of doing justice to a subject so glorious as this.

I have said enough for the end I have in view, which is, to make known the sentiments of love, respect, and praise, we ought to entertain towards this glorious Queen, for, from what I have laid down, it is abundantly evident that we should only attribute to her what is glorious, admirable, and sublime, as to grace, virtue, and all perfections and privileges; and that we should ever speak of her in conformity with such sentiments ; ever, in the highest and loftiest sense; ever, with the conviction that we can say nothing worthy of her, and that were men and angels to unite together, they would fail in sounding praises meet for the sublime dignity to which she has been raised.

Never let us listen, then, to other language than this; never let us forget the lesson taught by Gerson, the great Chancellor of Paris, that, in relation to Mary, one has only to dread falling into the mistake of speaking of her slightingly: when it becomes a question of praising her, the praises of men can never exceed, or even equal, her merits. It might be contended that it is our duty to limit our belief to what faith teaches, and to attribute to Mary nothing but what has a solid foundation in Scripture. Quite true ; but what more solid foundation than that of the Divine Maternity can possibly be desired ?

The Gospel says little about Mary, except that she is the Mother of Jesus.

"Certainly," exclaim the saints, "but in saying that much, it has said everything"—all the rest is included; it is only necessary to reason on this prerogative, in order to be able to say the most transcendent things about the Blessed Virgin; the foundation, the source, of every imaginable greatness is contained in this.

Here lie the principles from which endless conclusions may be drawn with regard to the glories of Mary; and from which, unceasingly, and to the end of time, new lights and fresh revelations may be deduced, according as the Holy Spirit in His all-wise designs may see fit more and more to enlighten the understandings of men.

We will conclude these chapters by considering what should be their fruit. If the respect and veneration due to any person is to be measured by his dignity, position, and power, all these being united in Mary to an incomparable extent, the homage and respect paid to her should be without limit.

On this point the doctrine of the Church is clear.

She assigns to Mary a worship which she calls "hyperdulian," that is to say, superior to that accorded to any angel or saint. The Blessed Virgin is placed in a position apart from all the rest; devotion to her should far exceed that to any other saint. As her dignity places her far above all other creatures, it is fitting that she should be honoured in due proportion.

What effect should belief in this truth produce in us? With what profound respect ought poor creatures like ourselves to be penetrated, in presence of this same Virgin? How should *we* approach her, to whom not even the most exalted spirits in heaven draw near without trembling? The highest of the seraphim falls prostrate, so to speak, at the feet of Mary, and shall men and sinners be only feebly struck by the glory of such exalted majesty?

In approaching, then, to pay your homage to Mary;—whenever you sing her praises, or offer her your prayers, reflect on what has been said, and never fail to experience in your inmost heart such a sentiment of respect, as shall make you acknowledge yourself to be as the dust under her feet.

You should feel yourself unworthy to be numbered amongst her servants, and happy to be allowed to approach her feet with the knowledge that she deigns to listen to your supplications and to receive your prayers.

This feeling of respect should extend to whatever relates to her; to her statues, and to places consecrated to her honour.

Whatever has any reference to her should, on that account, be treated with veneration. You will thus establish solidly in your souls that true devotion to the Blessed Virgin, of which a feeling of profound respect is the necessary foundation.

Hence will arise those other needful sentiments of confidence and love, concerning which we are about to speak.

CHAPTER IV.

ON CONFIDENCE IN THE BLESSED VIRGIN.

THE second point essential in devotion to Mary, is confidence, and that this is most conformable to the spirit of the Church, we shall now proceed to show, explaining, according to her interpretation, both its character and quality.

Confidence may be defined as the sweet and fervent hope of obtaining the assistance we desire, from the person to whom we have recourse. It is a reassuring conviction that our prayer, so far from being refused, will on the contrary be favourably received.

In this way would an obedient son approach the father or mother by whom he is tenderly loved, and who was in a position to grant his requests. So, too, would one friend have recourse to another ; so would a faithful servant demand assistance from a good and generous master.

To be able to place this confidence in any person, two qualities are necessary in him—power, and good-will.

He must possess the ability to assist, and must also be willing to do so.

The more one is persuaded that he has both these qualities, the greater does one's confidence in him become.

In order to excite perfect confidence in the Blessed Virgin, the power bestowed on her by God to assist us, and the good-will to do so with which He has inspired her, must be clearly pointed out.

Before entering upon this subject it will be well, however, for the benefit of less enlightened people, to remark, that some of the expressions employed by the Fathers of the Church, and even by the Church herself, denoting power and goodness appropriate only to Jesus, are to be understood in a very different sense when applied to the Blessed Virgin, to what they are when made use of in speaking of our Saviour. In saying, for instance, that the Blessed Virgin is "all-powerful," one does not attribute to her this perfection in the same sense as when alluding to her Divine Son.

Jesus derives from Himself His power and goodness; He is the source of these attributes: Mary has nothing of herself; whatever she receives comes from her Son: she is rich only in His gifts, and by His merits.

In the same way, when Mary receives the titles of Advocate, Mediator, and others suitable to Jesus, they are accorded to her in a sense far different from that which they would have if applied to Him.

To understand this, we must distinguish the two kinds of mediation; one, of merit and justice, the other, of grace and intercession. Jesus is our Mediator in the first sense; He made atonement for our sins; He only is, He only can be, our Mediator.

This is no reason why the Blessed Virgin should not with justice be called, in her special manner, the mediator of the human race; and on these three grounds—

First. Because in furnishing the body of the Saviour of the world, she abundantly gave her blood as the price of our redemption.

Second. Because she fully consented that this Son, Who belonged to her by every natural right, should die for the salvation of mankind; and hence, she suffered inconceivable sorrows which were most meritorious by reason of her exalted dignity.

Third. Because, in our behalf, she makes intercession before God more unceasingly than all the other saints; and her prerogative of Mother gives to her prayers that force and efficacy which render them capable of obtaining all they demand.

With these few remarks, I resume the subject.

On the power of the Blessed Virgin.

Has the Blessed Virgin much power in heaven to assist us in our wants?

This is one of those truths which reason, faith, and the Christian education received from earliest childhood, render so apparent and so evident; which is so deeply engraved in the minds and hearts of the faithful, that nothing is able to intensify its impression.

Has the Blessed Virgin much power in heaven?

The answer to such a question may be given in very few words.

Mary is the well-beloved Daughter of the Father, the Mother of the Son, equal to the Father in all things—the Spouse of the Holy Ghost.

She is the Queen of heaven and of earth.

Whoever pays attention to these words and fathoms their meaning, should be able to gain an idea of the power of Mary, which no sermons ever preached, no reasons ever offered, no books ever written, could possibly enlarge.

Mary, the daughter of the Eternal Father: this daughter so beloved, so free from blemish; after Jesus, the most perfect likeness of the Father; herself alone, more pleasing in His eyes than all other creatures together; the sweetest object, after Jesus, of the Divine complacency! What cannot such a daughter, reclining on the breast of such a Father, confidently hope to obtain?

Is it necessary to preach sermons in order that this may be understood?

Mary is the Mother of the Son; equal to His Father, and, like Him, God.

She is as truly His Mother, in the natural meaning and sense of the word, as they that bore us are our mothers.

Over this Son she exercises a natural right; one which is inseparably attached to the position of mother.

What can more powerfully influence the

heart of a good son, than the petition of his mother?

Are any other proofs needed? Mary is the Spouse of the Holy Ghost, which prerogative becomes her no less than the others. How can I give a more perfect notion of the supremacy of a princess at court, than by saying that she is the consort of the prince, the object of his tenderest regards, more dear to him than all the other members of his court, more precious than his whole kingdom?

Can any one demand further proofs of her being all-powerful with Him?

Mary is the Queen of heaven and earth; how can a more complete idea be given of her power in the kingdom of heaven, than by declaring that she is its Queen?

We must either pronounce the glorious titles accorded to Mary by the Church, and by the teaching of faith, to be vain and empty sounds; pompous and meaningless expressions (all which would be akin to blasphemy), or we must allow that the

Blessed Virgin is actually in possession of the power implied by her royal position, which is therefore practically unlimited. To go back to what I was saying: if Mary is the Queen of the universe, she undoubtedly possesses, unless this be a vain and empty title, the powers of a queen, and can confer benefits on her subjects, assisting them in all their necessities according to her good pleasure, and according to the pleasure of her Divine Son.

She is able to deliver them from the misfortunes by which they are surrounded, and which threaten them on every side, and it is in her power to make them happy. If not, of what avail would be her royalty? What! a queen unable to afford assistance to one in distress! Unable to obtain mercy for a criminal, unable to enrich a subject!

Is it likely, I ask, that the Queen of heaven should have less power in her kingdom than the queens of the earth possess in theirs? If Mary be indeed the Spouse of the Holy Ghost, and that such be not an empty name, she certainly possesses over Him the influence of a dearly-beloved Spouse. She is able to exercise over Him a gentle sway, to soften and turn aside His anger, and to obtain from Him numberless graces.

All these are the exclusive privileges of her position.

Finally, if Mary be in reality the Mother of Jesus, she exerts over the heart of the most tender and affectionate of sons all the influence which so perfect a Mother deserves to possess; that is to say, that over it she holds boundless sway.

These are truths, which, by their very simplicity, carry conviction to the mind, and so fully enlighten the understandings of all who attentively consider them, that no artifices of the enemies of Holy Church will ever succeed in obscuring them. Relying on these considerations, the Fathers and holy doctors of the

Church, when speaking of the might of the Blessed Virgin, do not hesitate to assert that "all power has been given to her, on earth and in heaven, to obtain whatever she desires."[1]

In like manner speaks Germain of Constantinople. "Over God you possess the influence of a mother, and it is impossible that your requests should ever be refused; for God, your Son, deigns to obey you in everything, as His pure and immaculate Mother."[2]

St. Bonaventure says, "Mary is the Queen of the angels in heaven, of men upon the earth, and of the devils in hell. O most powerful Queen, help us, who are unable to help ourselves."[3]

[1] Data est tibi omnis potestas in cœlo et in terra ut quidquid volueris valeas efficere. (St. Petr. Dam., Serm. de Nat.)

[2] Tu maternam vim apud Deum obtines nec enim fieri potest ut non exaudiaris, quoniam tibi ab omnia et per omnia et in omnibus tanquam caræ et immaculatæ matri obedit. (St. Germain, C. P. Serm. ii. de Dormit. Mar.)

[3] Maria, Domina angelorum in Cœlo, Domina hominum in mundo, et Domina dæmonum in

"Jesus Christ," says St. Bernard, "in redeeming the human race, made over the whole price to Mary."[1]

"Mary," adds Gerson, "has received the most perfect name which, after her Divine Son, any creature could possibly receive, viz., the august name of Mother of God. In virtue of this she holds dominion and exercises authority over the whole world, so that at her name all things bow down, in heaven, on earth, and in hell. In virtue of the same she has received fulness of grace, not only for herself, but on behalf of all mankind."[2] "No grace comes from heaven without passing through Mary's

inferno... O potentissima Domina, esto nobis impotentissimis auxiliatrix. (St. Bonav. in Speculo.)

[1] Christus redempturus humanum genus, pretium universum contulit in Mariam. (St. Bern., Serm. de Nat.)

[2] Domina nostra nomen accepit, perfectius quod esse possit homini post nomen Filii sui, est et quod Mater Dei dicatur. Per hoc habet veluti auctoritatem et naturale dominium ad totius mundi dominium ut in nomine suo omnia flectantur in cœlo et in terra et in inferno. Per hoc accepit plenitudinem gratiæ non solum pro se, sed et pro omnibus. (Gerson, de Annunt.)

hands."[1] But we are dwelling too long on a point with regard to which no one entertains a doubt.

What true Christian has ever doubted the power of the Mother of God?

We know she can do whatever she chooses; if she desires our salvation, and is willing to employ her power to obtain it, we have every reason to hope for happiness.

But will she desire it? Will not our sins and unworthiness prevent her from exercising her influence in our favour, and hinder her from interceding in our behalf?

Will not this Virgin, so pure, so holy, so full of zeal for the glory of her Son, be deterred by our iniquities and the outrages we have committed against Him?

This concerns the goodness of the Blessed Virgin towards us, and is the second quality which, as we have said, is a necessary part of true confidence. As is

[1] Nulla gratia venit de cœlo, nisi transeat per manus Mariæ. (Gerson, Serm. i., Nom. Mar.)

allowed by all the world, the Blessed Virgin has the power to assist us; but you ask if she has sufficient kindness of heart to wish to do so.

Is not the answer to this engraved on the hearts of the faithful? Can any one be found who doubts the goodness of the Blessed Virgin? Does any one exist to whom her mercies are so little known that he fails to be inspired with confidence in her?

Can any one inflict such an injury, O Mother of goodness and mercy, on thy tender heart? Does any one know so little of its compassion for men?

On the Goodness of the Blessed Virgin.

In order to form a sound judgment as to the goodness of the Blessed Virgin, there are certain principles which ought to serve for clear and unmistakable rules.

First. It is certain that Almighty God has endowed His Mother with every perfection, in such an eminent degree, that she far surpasses every other creature; whence it follows that in Mary is found more kindness of heart than exists in all men and saints and angels.

Second. It is equally certain that God, in creating Mary, has formed her to the most perfect image of the Divinity, and that she is the most complete and accurate expression of His perfections.

Now, as of all these mercy and compassion are the most prominent, according to the declaration of the prophet, "His mercies are above all His works,"[1]—so in the same proportion they should shine out amongst the other perfections of Mary and surpass them all.

Third. The Blessed Virgin is, without doubt, a perfect copy of her Son. No resemblance can be greater than that which exists between the Sacred Hearts of Mother and Son.

[1] Miserationes ejus super omnia opera ejus (Ps. cxliv.).

As the disposition of the Son moved Him to compassion for the sinners He died to save, it is very certain that the disposition of the Mother is similar to His.

Fourth and last principle. God, in creating Mary, destined her to become the Mother of the faithful. He therefore endowed her with a mother's heart in their regard; it was His will that she should be their advocate, their mediator, their refuge, their support, their consolation.

All this made it necessary that He should bestow on her, at the same time, an almost infinite yearning towards mercy.

These are sure and certain principles by which to judge concerning the goodness of Mary. It is enough to call attention to them without dwelling further on the matter, for in the hearts of the faithful there abides a sentiment more powerful than any argument.

You ask whether Mary is good enough to be willing to employ on our behalf all her power and influence. I answer, "Consult your heart."

A voice more powerful, more sweet, and more convincing than any words will tell you what you seek to know.

There you will find engraven a lively sentiment, inspired in earliest childhood, with regard to the mercies of Mary.

Call to mind the ideas instilled into you from the cradle, which you imbibed with the milk by which you were nourished.

You were taught to look upon her as your kind, good Mother; to call her by this endearing name, to run to her as children; you were taught to use the language of the whole Church, which bestows on her all the names so well suited for inspiring confidence — "Mother of mercy, Mother of grace, Comforter of the afflicted, Help and Hope of Christians and Refuge of sinners."

Have you forgotten all these loving titles which, day by day in the prayers addressed to Mary, were placed in your mouths by the Church of God?

Does this Holy Church deceive herself in attributing to Mary such qualities as these? Is it falsely and in vain that they have been bestowed upon her?

"Can we deny," asks St. Bernard, "that Mary sheds over all the world the light of Divine Wisdom and the dew of celestial grace?"[1] It is possible that you may be some great sinner, and that you doubt whether the mercy of Mary can extend as far as to you. Ah! my brother, whoever you may be, however great a sinner you may have become, however grievous your offences, if you wish to return to God, go to Mary! Her compassion extends even to you! Do not doubt it for one moment; she will receive you with love. Perhaps it is the only chance left to you, the one means, given you by God, for returning into the way of salvation!

But why seek for proofs of the mercy

[1] Dispensat divinæ sapientiæ lucem, et cœlestis gratiæ rorem. (St. Bern., Serm. iv. de Rom. Mar.)

of Mary towards sinners, when the universal Church desires us to regard her as their refuge?

"Refugium Peccatorum." Ah! what a consoling idea of her mercy and of her power is conveyed in this title! It is capable of exciting confidence even in the greatest sinners.

The Church, in bestowing it, alludes to those asylums of refuge where criminals are safe from the pursuit of human justice, if haply they succeed in gaining their shelter.

There no one can seize them; there they are secure from punishment, out of respect either for the place itself or for the powerful owner whose protection is implored.

According to the spirit of the Church, Mary is one of such places of refuge, open to poor sinners, where they can seek shelter when they desire to return to the grace of God.

In this asylum they are secured, as it

It is a sign of her compassion that they are permitted to find refuge with Mary, and a convincing proof of her surpassing influence that, with her, they are safe from the anger of Almighty God.

I take the case of a monarch who, in his just anger, pursues a rebellious subject; the unhappy and trembling culprit takes refuge with the mother of the king and implores her intercession; seeing this, the king himself, out of respect for his mother, pauses, listens to her petition, and, his anger being appeased, receives the offender again into favour.

Can the influence of a mother be shown to greater advantage?

This is the position of the Blessed Virgin with regard to her Son.

Behold! sinners, what the Church desires you to understand when she speaks of Mary as your refuge.

This sentiment, so glorious to Mary and so consoling to men, could be justified by numberless examples.

How many illustrious penitents could I mention who have found safety in this asylum, and who owe the forgiveness of their sins to the all-powerful intercession of Mary! I fearlessly include all converted sinners, and, like St. Bernard, defy any person to produce *one* who, "having had recourse to Mary, has not obtained relief." [1]

There have been abominable sinners—souls bound over to the devil—who, ready to despair at the sight of the enormity of their offences, have only been drawn back from the precipice by the hope that the Blessed Virgin would have compassion on them and make intercession on their behalf.

They have looked upon her as their only remaining hope; they have had recourse to her, and their confidence has never been misplaced. Mary, overflowing

---

[1] Sileat misericordiam tuam, Virgo Beata, si quis est qui invocatam te in suis necessitatibus, meminerit defuisse. (St. Bern., Serm. iv. de Assumpt.)

It is a sign of her compassion that they are permitted to find refuge with Mary, and a convincing proof of her surpassing influence that, with her, they are safe from the anger of Almighty God.

I take the case of a monarch who, in his just anger, pursues a rebellious subject: the unhappy and trembling culprit takes refuge with the mother of the king and implores her intercession; seeing this, the king himself, out of respect for his mother, pauses, listens to her petition, and his anger being appeased, receives him again into favour.

Can the influence of to greater advantage

CHAPTER V.

...RISTICS OF CONFIDENCE IN ...LESSED VIRGIN.

...been already said must be ...ervations on the character- ...ccording to the spirit of the ... be included in

... to three. Our ... of God should ... full of affection

...ACTERISTIC.

...niversal, that is to say, ...course to the Blessed ..., in every place, and in ...hether temporal o...

with compassion for sinners, has received them with kindness, and obtained for them the pardon they desired.

Many wonderful instances are recorded of sinners who have been rescued by Mary from the very gates of hell, the history of which, written by authors of undoubted repute, are startling proofs of the compassion of this Divine Mother, and of the power which she possesses in heaven.

CHAPTER V.

ON THE CHARACTERISTICS OF CONFIDENCE IN THE BLESSED VIRGIN.

To what has been already said must be added a few observations on the characteristics which, according to the spirit of the Church of God, ought to be included in confidence in Mary.

They may be reduced to three. Our confidence in the Mother of God should be universal, continual, and full of affection and tenderness.

First Characteristic.

It ought to be universal, that is to say, we should have recourse to the Blessed Virgin at all times, in every place, and in all necessities, whether temporal or spiritual; whether of soul or body, whether relating to this life or to the next; whether for ourselves, our neighbours, or our friends.

And why is this? It is because the power and compassion of Mary embrace all these conditions, extend to all times and to every place, and apply to all sorts of needs and to all kinds of persons.

"Who," cries St. Bernard, "can measure the length, and the breadth, and the height, and the depth of the mercy of Mary?"

Its length extends through every century; its breadth includes the whole wide world; its height stretches even to the vaults of heaven; its depth carries it down to the very dungeons of hell.

Such is the standard by which we must measure our confidence; thus have the saints measured theirs, as is evident from the expressions they employ.

Such also, and above all, is the spirit of the Church of God, a consideration full of consolation.

The Church, whose conduct—always holy, always conformable to the Spirit of Jesus Christ—must be our infallible guide, recognises so clearly in Mary the power and goodwill of which we are speaking, that she herself repairs to this Divine Advocate in all her needs and on behalf of each one of her children.

This is clearly shown in the prayers which she addresses to her, and in which she claims her assistance for all.

"Holy Mary, succour the miserable, aid the weak, comfort the afflicted, pray for the people, assist the clergy, intercede for the devout female sex; let all who invoke thee feel the effects of thy protection."[1]

I hear this holy Church beseeching Mary to grant deliverance from all evils and from every danger. "We fly to thy patronage, O Holy Mother of God, despise

---

[1] Sancta Maria, succurre miseris, juva pusillanimes, refove flebiles, ora pro populo, interveni pro clero, intercede pro devoto femineo sexu; sentiant omnes tuam juvamen, quicumque celebrant tuam sanctam commemorationem.

Does this Holy Church deceive herself in attributing to Mary such qualities as these ? Is it falsely and in vain that they have been bestowed upon her?

"Can we deny," asks St. Bernard, "that Mary sheds over all the world the light of Divine Wisdom and the dew of celestial grace?"[1] It is possible that you may be some great sinner, and that you doubt whether the mercy of Mary can extend as far as to you. Ah! my brother, whoever you may be, however great a sinner you may have become, however grievous your offences, if you wish to return to God, go to Mary! Her compassion extends even to you! Do not doubt it for one moment; she will receive you with love. Perhaps it is the only chance left to you, the one means, given you by God, for returning into the way of salvation!

But why seek for proofs of the mercy

[1] Dispensat divinæ sapientiæ lucem, et cœlestis gratiæ rorem. (St. Bern., Serm. iv. de Rom. Mar.)

of Mary towards sinners, when the universal Church desires us to regard her as their refuge?

"Refugium Peccatorum." Ah! what a consoling idea of her mercy and of her power is conveyed in this title! It is capable of exciting confidence even in the greatest sinners.

The Church, in bestowing it, alludes to those asylums of refuge where criminals are safe from the pursuit of human justice, if haply they succeed in gaining their shelter.

There no one can seize them; there they are secure from punishment, out of respect either for the place itself or for the powerful owner whose protection is implored.

According to the spirit of the Church, Mary is one of such places of refuge, open to poor sinners, where they can seek shelter when they desire to return to the grace of God.

In this asylum they are secured, as it

not our petitions in our necessities, but deliver us always from all dangers, O ever-glorious and Blessed Virgin.[1]

Witness the prayers which the Church addresses to Mary, the antiphons, the hymns in the missal and in the divine office, in short, all the prayers she teaches the faithful. This universal confidence of which I speak is to be found throughout.

From the Blessed Virgin, as from one who of right dispenses them, she begs for all her children the richest graces. "Break our fetters; rescue us from the blindness of sin; deliver us from all our miseries; obtain for us every good gift."[2]

She implores "innocence, final perseverance, possession of God, and life everlasting."[3]

---

[1] Sub tuum præsidium confugimus, sancta Dei genitrix : nostras deprecationes ne despicias in necessitatibus; sed à periculis cunctis libera nos semper, Virgo gloriosa et benedicta.

[2] Solve vincla reis, profer lumen cæcis, mala nostra pelle, bona cuncta posce.

[3] Vitam præsta puram, iter para tutum, ut videntes Jesum semper collætemur.

Notice, also, that she supplicates these graces from Mary in a very different manner from that in which she addresses the other saints. She demands them from Mary as from their dispenser, as from one, in fact, who holds them ready in her hands.

With regard to the other saints, the Church employs for the most part such expressions as these, " Pray for us; intercede for us." With regard to Mary, she frequently and plainly says, "Give us; vouchsafe to us; deliver us; save us; have pity on us. Show thyself a mother to us; obtain from Him who for us deigned to become thy Son, the reception of our prayers through thee."[1]

This universal power of the Blessed Virgin is so well recognised by the Church that, for every kind of grace, its members apply to her as to the source from which they flow.

[1] Monstra te esse matrem, sumat per te preces, qui pro nobis natus tulit esse tuus.

The Church, throughout the world, honours her by every conceivable title which may animate the confidence of her children. She calls her "Notre Dame de Consolation," and honours her in many churches and chapels under this title. This she does out of regard for such as are afflicted. In other places she is invoked as "Notre Dame de Miséricorde;" this, again, is for the sake of those who are afflicted in mind or body. Here she is invoked under the title of "Notre Dame d'Espérance," as a remedy against despair; there, under that of "Notre Dame de Grâce," as an antidote to temptation to sin. She is called "Notre Dame du Refuge," against the persecutions of our enemies, visible and invisible; "Notre Dame de Paix," in opposition to all trouble and discord; "Notre Dame de Lumière," as opposed to the darkness of ignorance and error; "Notre Dame de Bon-Secours," as against the abandonment of creatures; "Notre Dame de Remède," as ministering to sickness of soul or body;

"Notre Dame des Agonisans," as the patroness of a happy death; " Notre Dame Libératrice," as fighting against the captivity of the people and the tyranny of men; "Notre Dame de la Victoire," as the strength of Christian armies; "Notre Dame de Bon-Rencontre; Notre Dame de Tout-Pouvoir," in order to designate her power. Thus, too, of the other titles applied to Mary, which are all well calculated to excite confidence and bring great consolation to the hearts of the faithful.

All these beautiful titles convey better than any explanation the opinion held by the Church as to the limitless power conferred by Jesus on His Divine Mother, and they must teach us to look to her for all the benefits they suggest.

Thence springs the universal desire of Mary's patronage, witnessed throughout the Church in all ages, in every condition, and in each country where the Christian religion is known.

This same devotion is common to men

and women, to great and small, to the just and to sinners, to kings and to their subjects, to priests and to the laity, to religious and to seculars.

In every age, and sex, and condition how many true servants of Mary are to be found, specially devoted to her, and who constantly carry about with them some outward token of their love and confidence —rosary, scapular, image, or medal!

Where is the priest or pastor of a flock who does not make it his duty to exhort his hearers to place themselves under the protection of Mary?

What religious body is to be found which does not look upon Mary as its Mother and its foundress?

What king neglects to invoke her as the Protectress of his kingdom, his person, and his family?

France! the piety of thy kings presents itself to my mind and arrests my attention. Thou hast witnessed thy powerful and devoted monarchs placing their crowns and sceptres at Mary's feet, recognising her for their sovereign, and consecrating to her by special vows their person and their kingdom.

Each year it was their custom to renew this offering at the foot of her altar, and to issue commands that through the length and breadth of their domains this engagement of theirs should be made known to all the people and celebrated with due solemnity.

It was their desire that, on this solemn occasion, the highest and noblest in the land should follow their example and publicly offer to the Queen of heaven their respectful homage and proofs of their devotion to her service.

Happy France! what mayst thou not expect from the protection of the Mother of God? No kingdom, in ages gone by, has shown more zeal for her glory than thou; none has produced more illustrious defenders of her privileges.

For the sake of thy happiness, Heaven

grant that this zeal may never be wanting to thee, and that heresy—so hateful to Mary—may never intervene to destroy or weaken thy devotion to her.

Mother of God, turn away this evil from us, and ever regard, with eyes of favour and compassion, a kingdom so specially consecrated to thee.

Look favourably upon the monarch who, following the footsteps of his predecessors, affords thee such open proofs of his homage and veneration. Deign to receive him under thy protection; make him worthy to bear the names of "Eldest Son of the Church," and "Most Christian King;" fill him with ardent zeal for thy glory; and such will be a certain token of the Divine favours by which his reign will be made happy.

I return now to the subject of that general confidence in the Blessed Virgin which is so noticeable in the Church.

To whom do we fly, in all our corporal

or spiritual necessities, with more confidence than we do to Mary?

Who but Mary is sought by all sinners, in order that they may obtain pardon for their offences?

Mary is their refuge—"Refugium Peccatorum." To whom do those address themselves who are in sorrow and affliction unless to Mary, the Comforter of the afflicted—"Consolatrix afflictorum"?

In the wants that so often press upon them, whose but Mary's help do all Christians seek? The Church calls her the Help of Christians—"Auxilium Christianorum."

In dangers by land or sea, who is invoked with more confidence or affection than Mary?

In public calamities, such as war, pestilence, and famine, who but Mary is had recourse to, in order that by her intercession the scourges of Divine justice may be turned aside?

Where is the kingdom, or province, or

city which would not, at such times as these, be solemnly dedicated and consecrated to Mary?

So deeply is confidence in this powerful mediator engraved in all hearts, that even when accidents happen so sudden as to give no time for thought, in all cases of pressing need, when one instinctively calls on God, Mary is invoked in the same breath and summoned to render assistance —"O my God! O Blessed Virgin! aid me, save me!"

Here, then, is the first characteristic of confidence in Mary: it must be universal. The necessity of this is well emphasised by the conduct of the Church, and by that spirit which, as we have seen, is so widely spread amongst her children.

Second Characteristic.

It must be continual.

It is not enough to seek assistance from the Blessed Virgin only from time to time, on her most important feasts, on certain days consecrated in her honour, in certain important actions, in certain pressing necessities. No, no, this is not enough. This confidence must be evinced on all occasions, each day and every hour; and this because, on the one hand, we are in continual want of help, and, on the other, because God takes pleasure in relieving our necessities through Mary. Here again I will follow the example given us by the Church, inspired by the Holy Spirit which guides her.

She demands nothing of God without employing the mediation of Mary.

In all her masses, in all her offices, in all her ceremonies, in all the prayers she offers, on every occasion, she invokes Mary. Open any of the books employed for the Holy Sacrifice, on which page is not the name of Mary inscribed?

Turn over the leaves of any ritual, the orders for conducting the most solemn and holy functions, benedictions, consecrations, or administrations of the sacraments, the name of Mary is to be discovered throughout; she is continually invoked, and her intercession constantly implored.

It would appear that, as the Eternal Father has willed that the Church should offer no petition except through the merits of His Divine Son, so it has been the desire of the Son that in all our wants our prayers should come to Him through Mary.

It is in this spirit that the Church commences each hour in the divine office by an invocation to Mary, concluding each in the same way, with an anthem sung in her honour.

There is no mass in which Mary is not several times solemnly invoked; three times a day, at the sound of the Angelus bell, the Church warns the faithful to pronounce her name. She approves the general custom which, in every sermon, allows invocations to Mary to mingle with the Divine Word; and each month in the year is filled with different feasts in her honour; thus rendering devotion to the Mother of God well-nigh continual.

Remark the care which the Church takes to inspire all her children, young and old, with this spirit of confidence.

No sooner can a child begin to speak than he is taught to pronounce and to invoke the name of Mary at the same time as that of Jesus, and never to separate these holy names.

No sooner is he able to pray than he is instructed, at the same time as he addresses the "Our Father" to God, to lisp the "Hail Mary" in honour of the Blessed Virgin; the Church being well convinced that any prayer presented by Mary will be well received by God.

No sooner are the faithful in a proper state to receive instructions than, after teaching them to know, to love, and to serve Jesus as their Lord and Saviour, she teaches them also to reverence Mary as the Mother of God, and to invoke her constantly as their mediator in all their wants.

At morning and evening devotions, at mass, confession, and communion, in the church and at home, in almost every prayer made use of for the sanctification of daily life, the name of Mary is employed.

The books of devotion placed in the hands of the faithful, and all the prayers in most general use, are full of the praises of Mary, and abound in invocations for her assistance.

Rosaries, litanies, little offices, hymns, antiphons, and many pious formulæ by which to consecrate oneself to Mary, and merit her protection—these are the means by which the Church nourishes the devotion of her children.

It is the holy will of God that no novelties should supplant these practices consecrated by the piety of our fathers.

The zeal of the Church in exciting devotion to Mary is still further evidenced by the favours with which she loads all those who assiduously invoke her name.

How many confraternities have been established in honour of the Blessed Virgin, how many congregations and holy assemblies have been approved!

How many graces have been accorded, how many privileges and indulgences vouchsafed!

Never is the Church more liberal than when she desires to induce her children to honour and invoke Our Lady, in consequence of which, no practice is more common amongst them than this.

Here we see, what the second characteristic of our confidence ought to be.

It ought to be continual.

There yet remains a third, which should perfect both the others: our confidence should be ardent and full of tenderness and affection; ardent, in proportion as we are needy and desire assistance; affectionate, in accordance with the character of her whom we invoke.

Let us take example once more from the Church. Nothing can exceed the earnestness, the affection, and the tenderness she evinces in the prayers which she addresses to Mary, and in the devout practices which she consecrates to her.

Throughout this holy Church, which spreads over all the world, you will everywhere perceive her tenderness, devotion, and love in all that relates to Mary.

What feasts are there, always excepting those of our Blessed Lord, that draw together larger congregations, or excite more fervour and devotion, than those of Mary?

What churches are more frequented than those dedicated to Our Lady?

What confraternities are more extended or more numerous than those established in her honour?

Whose praises are more willingly listened to in the holy choirs than the praises of Mary?

What sanctuaries are more famous for the crowds of pilgrims and worshippers by which they are thronged than those consecrated to her, and which by the special providence of God are scattered so widely throughout the Christian world?

What statues of devotion are more generally seen, more commonly honoured, than those of Mary? They are found not only in the churches, where they are placed on almost every altar, but also in private dwellings; for who has not, in his house, or chamber, or oratory, some statue or picture of the Blessed Virgin?

Her holy image is to be seen in public places—over the doors of public buildings, over the gates of the city, along the principal highways; it is everywhere presented to the eyes of the faithful as the most tender object of their confidence and love.

What name, after the Holy Name of Jesus, is so often on the lips and in the earts of the faithful as the name of

Mary? These two holy names are inseparable—"Jesus and Mary." They are always associated together in the mouths of faithful Christians during life and at the hour of death, in the midst of prosperity or in the hour of adversity, in times of danger and temptation.

This holy name is like a precious balm to soothe our woes; it is the unfailing remedy in all maladies of the soul; it is a powerful weapon against all the enemies of our salvation.

But, it may be asked, is there no danger that this confidence in Mary, so strongly recommended,(and so enduring, might interfere with the confidence we ought to have in Jesus, who, after all, is our true Mediator, our Divine Advocate with the Eternal Father, the undoubted Author of our salvation, and the Source of every grace which we receive?

Why should we seek assistance from any one but Him? Has He not more love for us than Mary has, more power to help us?

Why not go direct to Him in preference to any another?

In order to satisfy these objections which might occur to simple souls, and which heretics employ in order to destroy *all* devotion to the Blessed Virgin and to the saints, we will make the following observations:—

First. If in this argument there be any real weight, it would at once put an end to all invocation of the saints, which is nevertheless an article of faith in the Catholic Church.

Why address any but Jesus alone? Is not He sufficient in Himself? Is the saint you invoke more powerful than He is to assist you?

A principle which thus destroys a practice founded on faith is a false and erroneous one.

Second. Observe the wisdom of that providence which guides the Church.

God wills that His saints should be honoured, and that there should be a perfect union between the Church triumphant in heaven and militant on earth.

On our part, this union consists in the honour we pay to the saints, and the invocations we employ to obtain their intercession; on their part, in the favourable hearing they give us, God having bestowed on them the power of obtaining for us all necessary graces.

Such is the conduct of God towards the saints. He desires that they should be highly esteemed in the Church, and employs the most efficacious means for bringing this about, by causing the graces we need to be received through them.

This order of things He has been pleased to establish, and it concerns above all others the Blessed Virgin, whom He has distinguished above the rest, and constituted the universal dispenser of His graces.

This in no manner derogates from His goodness or His power: not from His goodness, for it is a sweet proof of His affection that He should provide for us such a pleasant path by which we may approach Him; not from His power, for well we know that all things proceed from Him, and that the Blessed Virgin only passes on to us what she has received from Him on our behalf. So far, then, from diminishing our love for Jesus and our confidence in Him, this ought, on the contrary, to increase and strengthen them.

Let us add to these reflections an example which will embrace them all and render them more apparent.

A mighty king, animated by affection for his subjects, dearly loves his queen, who is ornamented with all the brightest virtues and every noble quality.

In order to satisfy his love for her he commands that his subjects should pay her all the homage they are capable of rendering. To this end he appoints for her a throne close to his own, he enriches her with every treasure and ornament he possesses, and causes her to become, to the fullest extent in his power, an object of admiration and respect.

Besides all this, he endows her with complete influence over himself, makes her the dispenser of all his favours, and causes it to be universally proclaimed throughout the kingdom that he has bestowed on her this privilege, commanding at the same time that his subjects shall apply to her whenever they have any petitions to make.

From every corner of the kingdom these approach their queen, and the king views with delight the crowds which throng round her, and the confidence they show in her power, that confidence which he himself has been at so much pains to excite.

Through her he receives all their requests, refusing none which she chooses to present.

Here I must pause to ask two questions.

First. Does the conduct of this king take away from his glory, or from the love he bears his subjects?

Second. Would it, in such a case as

this, betoken any want of confidence in the king, or show any disrespect towards him, if his subjects paid their addresses to the queen?

If one of these were to be reproached for addressing himself to any but the king alone; would such a reproach be well founded?

What answer ought to be given to such a blind accuser? Would not the very children reply, "We go to the queen because the king tells us to do so, he wishes to be approached through her"?

The application of this example to our Dear Lord and His Blessed Mother is obvious. This conduct of Almighty God towards all the saints, but particularly towards the Blessed Virgin, is so generally recognised in the Church, that whoever desires to obtain any special favour, asks it through her, or through one of the other saints.

Say, for instance, that the cure of an invalid, the success of an undertaking, or relief from some misfortune is desired, what course is generally pursued?

Each one, as he may be led by his particular devotion and by the inspiration of Divine grace, repairs to one of the saints, to St. Joseph, St. John, St. Anthony of Padua, St. Francis of Sales, St. Regius, or St. Theresa.

This is the universal practice of the faithful; but, as we have before observed, to whom amongst the saints do we have recourse so frequently as to the Blessed Virgin?

This conduct, so general throughout the Church of God, is an evident sign of the Spirit of Christ who is her guide.

Should you, therefore, ask me whether confidence in Mary is not calculated to weaken that which we owe to Jesus, I answer "No! for such is the Divine will of our Dear Lord Himself in appointing His Mother to be our advocate and our mediator. No! for she is the path by which it is His holy pleasure that we should come to Him. No! for such is the conduct which the Church employs, and which she teaches her faithful children. No! for the greatest saints, filled with the Spirit of God, have shown us this example."

There are none who have not been full of confidence in Mary. St. Cyril, St. Anselm, St. Bernard, St. Dominic, St. Francis of Assisi, St. Ignatius, all the founders of religious Orders, St. Theresa, St. Catherine, St. Mary Magdalen of Pazzi, and, in a word, every saint in heaven.

You cannot point to a single one whose love and confidence were not notorious. The most illustrious servants of Jesus have been the most faithful servants of Mary.

But speak Thyself, O Saviour of the world; I venture to seek evidence from Thee in a matter so deeply interesting to Thy Sacred Heart, so much the object of Thy love.

Speak, Thyself, O Lord, and let us

know whether the sentiments we are endeavouring to excite towards Thy Blessed Mother are pleasing to Thee, and in accordance with Thy holy will, or whether in publishing them abroad to the world we have fallen into error.

If indeed we be mistaken, I am bold enough, O Lord, to declare that it is Thou Thyself who hast led us astray; for it is by the constant miracles Thou ceasest not to work in favour of such as invoke Thy Mother, that so great confidence in her is kept alive.

Thou hast filled the world with miracles, the results of her intercession!

It is Thy word; it is Thy testimony!

Thou hast sounded a mighty voice in every corner of the globe, and, not content to proclaim by the mouths of Thy servants and by Thy Holy Church the bounty of Thy Mother towards mankind, and the power with which Thou hast endowed her for their assistance, Thou hast wonderfully acted upon men, in the manner most fitted sensibly to touch their hearts, and hast accorded the richest graces, spiritual as well as temporal, to such as have called upon her name!

Look back upon every age and time since Christianity was first established, traverse each district and kingdom, all the provinces and towns where Christians are to be found, or where they have ever been gathered together,—what clime so remote and uncivilised that a shrine in honour of Mary is nowhere to be found within it, a shrine famous for miracles which have been performed at her intercession?

What spot on the surface of the world has not been distinguished on account of some great benefit obtained through the intercession of this august Queen?

Through her, what maladies have been cured, how many of those possessed have obtained relief, how many dead have been restored to life, how many tempests have been stilled, how many shipwrecks averted, how many victories gained, how many wars brought to an end, how many woes and scourges of Divine justice have been turned aside!

With regard also to spiritual graces, how many sinners have been converted, how many heresies extirpated, how many temptations overcome, how many helps obtained!

The holy memorials with which the piety and gratitude of the people have enriched her shrines, bear faithful witness to the marvellous results of the all-powerful patronage of the Mother of God.

Through how many centuries has God worked miracles in every country, on behalf of those who seek assistance from Mary!

In order to establish His Church He worked miracles without end; how many has He performed in order to promulgate devotion to His Blessed Mother!

And can we yet doubt whether the confidence we place in this Queen of heaven is pleasing in His sight?

Let us conclude this consideration with

a beautiful saying of St. Bernard, at the same time remembering the views which have always been entertained by the saints as to the confidence we ought to place in the Blessed Virgin.

See how this great saint in his day exhorted the faithful to have recourse to Mary, and let his words be deeply impressed upon your hearts.

"Ah! my brethren," cried this holy doctor, in speaking of the dignity and mercy of Our Lady, "let us go, let us hasten to Mary; let us run to her with all the affection of which our hearts are capable, with all the strength of the utmost love by which we can be animated."

But no words can adequately render those in the original Latin, which are as follows :—" Totis ergo medullis cordium, totis præcordiorum affectibus ac votis omnibus Mariam hanc veneremur."[1]

What life, what tenderness, what fervour in these expressions! He desires that our

[1] St. Bern., de Aquæductu.

hearts should be penetrated to the core with confidence in Mary, "totis medullis cordium;" that we should be moved to the inmost depths of our being, "totis præcordiorum affectibus;" that our most solemn vows should be made in her regard, "ac votis omnibus."

But why should we thus repair with such ardour and such confidence to Mary?

Attend to the reason given by this holy doctor, who was in an especial manner enlightened as to the glories and the dignities of Mary.

"It is," he tells us, "because it is the will of God, who has designed that we should receive through her hands every good gift of which we stand in need."[1]

"O man," he continues, "whoever you may be, who have discovered that this life resembles rather a stormy sea, whereon we rise and fall, the sport of the angry waves,

---

[1] Quia sic est voluntas Dei, qui totum nos habere voluit per Mariam. (St. Bern., Serm. ii. Super Missus.)

than the solid earth on which we can securely tread: if you wish to escape shipwreck, turn your eyes towards Mary; fix your regards on her. She is the star of hope, and is ready to be your guide."[1]

"If temptations, like so many angry winds, should rise around you; if you find yourself in trouble and in danger of perishing, look up to that star; call on Mary."[2]

"Should you be agitated by motions of pride, ambition, calumny, or envy, look up to that star; call on Mary."[3]

"Should anger, avarice, or passion place your bark in peril, look up to Mary."[4]

---

[1] O quisquis te intelligis in hujus seculi profluvio magis inter procellas et tempestates fluctuare quam per terram ambulare; ne avertas oculos a fulgore hujus sideris, si non vis obrui procellis. (Ibid.)

[2] Si insurgant venti tentationum, si incurras sæpulos afflictionum, respice stellam, voca Mariam. (Ibid.)

[3] Si jactaris superbia undis, si ambitionis, si detractionis, si æmulationis, respice stellam, voca Mariam. (Ibid.)

[4] Si iracundia, aut avaritia, aut carnis illecebra naviculam concusserit mentis, respice ad Mariam. (Ibid.)

"If the horror occasioned by the enormity of your crimes should bring trouble to your soul ; if, terrified by the judgments of the Almighty, sorrow should take possession of your heart, and you should find yourself drifting into the gulf of despair, think on Mary."[1]

"In all dangers and misfortunes, and in every evil that befalls you, think on Mary; invoke Mary; let her name be ever in your heart and on your lips."[2]

The saint concludes with these words, which, together with those just quoted, form part of the office of the Holy Name of Mary. Would they were engraved in every heart!

"Follow Mary," he says, "and you will never go astray; pray to her and you will not be disappointed. Upheld by her, you

---

[1] Si criminum immensitate turbatus, conscientiæ fœditate confusus, judicii horrore perterritus barathro incipias absorberi tristitiæ, desperationis abysso, cogita Mariam. (Ibid.)

[2] In periculis, in angustiis, in rebus dubiis, Mariam cogita, Mariam invoca, non recedat ab ore, non recedat à corde. (Ibid.)

will never fall; as long as she protects you, you need have no fear; if she leads you, the road will become easy to your feet." [1]

"If only she be with you, you will safely reach the port for which you are bound; you will enter the harbour of everlasting life."

Is it a man who thus expresses himself, or the Holy Spirit of God?

[1] Ipsam sequens, non devias; ipsam rogans, non desperas; ipsâ tenente, non corruis; ipsâ protegente non metuis; ipsâ duce, non fatigaris. (Ibid.)

CHAPTER VI.

ON LOVE FOR THE BLESSED VIRGIN.

THE third and most important characteristic of devotion to the Blessed Virgin is love for her. This is the fruitful source of zeal for her glory, and the origin of every honour that is paid her.

Love of Mary is one of the most precious gifts of grace; all the saints possessed it; it is a sweet and certain sign of predestination.

Predestinating grace inspires this love in the hearts of the elect; it is a fruit which, as it were, always accompanies grace, and is its natural result.

Mary, being the Mother of the elect, all who have the felicity of being of that number must love her as sons.

Those who never feel any love for Our

Lady, who are cold and indifferent in her service, and despise all the practices established in her honour, bear, on the contrary, and in the same degree, the marks of reprobation; for, as it is a fact that all the saints have loved Mary, so also is it true that all who have been considered reprobate by the Church—such as founders of heresies—have invariably looked upon her with aversion, and refused to render her their homage.

Let us consider how this love belongs to Mary by right.

There is a love founded on esteem and preference; there is also one of sentiment and affection.

In devotion to Mary these two kinds of love should be inseparable; for, after her adorable Son, she is deserving of both in a sovereign degree.

The love which springs from esteem and preference is founded on the perfections of the person who is loved, on his dignity, power, holiness, wisdom, bounty, &c. This kind of love is due to him in proportion as he surpasses others in the possession of such perfections.

The love born of sentiment and affection rests on those amiable qualities of sweetness, clemency, liberality, and the like, which naturally excite in the heart feelings of sensible affection.

This kind of love is also based on certain ties and sympathies, which have the effect of closely uniting hearts together.

A mother, a wife, a friend, or a benefactor is thus loved with a sensible affection. The more such qualities as those alluded to are multiplied in the same person, the more richly he is endowed with them, the more does our love for him increase. In the same way, the closer our relationship with any one, the more loving are the feelings we entertain towards him. This sentimental love has different degrees, and is capable of being indefinitely intensified in proportion as the motives producing it become more powerful.

In this double sense is Almighty God loved even in this life by His saints, according to the degree in which He manifests to them His perfections.

That love, produced by the esteem and preference to which He is entitled, is commanded to all. Sensible love is a free gift which He bestows, according to His good pleasure, and in such abundance as He chooses, on those whom it is His holy will thus to favour; and it is undoubtedly true that souls distinguished in this manner have sometimes been deluged to such an extent by the sensible love of God, that it has produced in their hearts effects of tenderness and affection more wonderful than profane love—even the most ardent —is capable of understanding.

To come now to the Blessed Virgin.

She deserves this twofold love of esteem and of affection, and can never be loved to the full extent that is her due.

On the one hand, her merits and perfections surpass all created intelligence;

and on the other, the endearing qualities of which she is possessed, and the ties by which we are bound to her, are more fitted than any others to excite and inflame in our hearts feelings of sensible love.

Let us throw a little light on these two considerations.

On the love founded on esteem which is due to the Blessed Virgin.

If the love which springs from esteem depends on the perfections of the person we love, and should be proportionate to their excellence and number, to what point should not be carried the love due to the Blessed Virgin, her perfections, whether as to their number or their excellence, being equalled by nothing in the whole range of creation?

St. Thomas, that master of theology, teaches us that the perfections of Mary must be proportionate to her dignity as Mother of God.

In this sentence every thing is contained. Her dignity being infinite, her perfections can be limited by no finite bounds; whence it follows that if you were able to unite all the perfections of angels and of men, even all of them together would fail to approach those with which the Blessed Virgin is adorned.

She is incomprehensible even to the highest of the Seraphim, who, in consequence, can never love her to the full extent which she deserves.

Her Divine Son alone can adequately love her, for He alone can fully understand what she is.

She is so deserving of love that no mere creature can love her half enough; her merits eclipsing those of all the angels and saints, as much as the radiance of the moon dims the lustre of the surrounding stars.

This love, then, so much her due, ought to supersede every other affection.

Should any one fear that in language like this the Blessed Virgin is placed too nearly in the position of her Divine Son, and that there is danger of confounding the greatness of the one with that of the other, it can only be from want of consideration.

Whilst such an infinite distance separates them, how can any doubt be entertained that the Mother is placed too near the Son? Who is ignorant of the fact that, whilst the perfections of the Son are infinite, those of the Mother proceed from Him?

There is, in truth, an infinite distance between them; a distance which forbids all idea of that sort of equality which, as we are supposing, might possibly be feared. But the mind must be strangely distorted, the heart but poorly disposed, that can conjure up difficulties like these!

That they should be found amongst heretics excites no surprise, for these the devil inspires with some portion of the hatred he himself bears this Immaculate Virgin; that any Catholics should entertain such ideas would indeed be most astonishing. In attributing to the Blessed Virgin perfections approaching the infinite, the expressions made use of must not be taken in an extreme sense.

They are employed in order to indicate a greatness and superexcellence which passes the comprehension of angels and of men, in order to bring home to the mind that the difference, in point of dignity, between the Blessed Virgin and any other created being, is so immense that, for want of other terms, such words as "infinite," "immense," and "incomprehensible," are necessarily used in order to explain it at all; it being taken for granted that the faithful perfectly understand in what sense to receive such expressions and the limits which should be assigned to them. It would here be well to make an important reflection.

In assigning to the Blessed Virgin perfections which so far surpass all created intelligence, to whom does the principa glory revert?

Is it to the Blessed Virgin, or to her Divine Son?

Is it the Blessed Virgin who has made herself so holy, so full of wisdom, so powerful, so perfect, and so glorious; or is all this the work of her Son?

Can any one be so blind as to be unable to perceive this?

"Whatever is said in honour of the Mother," cries St. Bernard, "applies to the Son; all the praises bestowed on her belong to Him." [1]

Arnould de Chartres expresses the same idea in still more forcible language.

"It is not enough," he says, "to assert that the Son shares all His glory with the Mother, I protest that it is the same glory rather than one common to them both." [1]

Whenever we publish the glory of Mary, we are at the same time telling the glory of God.

The glory of the workman consists in the excellence of his work.

[1] Quidquid in laudibus Matris proferimus, ad Filium pertinet. (St. Bern., Serm. Sup. Missus.)
[1] Filii gloriam cum Matre, non tam communem judico quam eamdem. (St. Bern., de Laud. Mariæ.)

Take away from the glory of Mary, and you at the same time detract from the glory of the Great Author of her being.

The more sublime her dignity, the more does the power of God shine forth.

All the glory of the well-beloved Son of the Eternal Father proceeds from the Father; all the grandeur of this Mother of the Eternal Word proceeds from her Son.

All the grandeur of this Spouse of the Holy Ghost is His transcendent gift.

Whatever, then, is said in honour of Mary, is said in honour of the Father, and of the Son, and of the Holy Ghost, whom it has pleased to render this Daughter, this Mother, this Spouse, an object of admiration in heaven and upon the earth.

If any one is distressed by what seems to him excessive praise of the Blessed Virgin, it can only be from his want of enlightenment as to the sublime dignity of the Mother of the Creator: Almighty

God, whose holy will it was to render the Sacred Humanity of Jesus Christ the masterpiece of His magnificence and His bounty, who exhausted all His treasures in order to make the Word Incarnate the incomprehensible object of adoration both to angels and to men, has also ordained that the Mother of this His Son should have a share in His infinite glory, proportionate to her dignity as Mother.

He has made of her another masterpiece of His power, His greatness, and His bounty; inferior, it is true, to the first in created perfections, but so far removed above any other that words expressive of her glory and exaltation are altogether wanting.

Let this, in conclusion, be a rule in considering to what extent the love which is born of esteem is due to the Blessed Virgin.

She deserves to be loved above every other creature in heaven and on earth, above all but God Himself; she alone is to be prized above all the saints and angels together; in a word, after her Son, it is impossible ever to feel for her enough of this love of esteem and preference.

O God! graciously shed Thy light upon these words of mine, and grant that we may be able to realise the greatness and excellence of this Virgin, whom it has pleased Thee to raise to the dignity of being Thy Mother.

To convey any adequate idea of this surpassing greatness, our expressions must still remain powerless indeed.

ON THE LOVE OF AFFECTION AND TENDERNESS DUE TO THE BLESSED VIRGIN.

This love is founded, on the one hand, on the endearing qualities before noticed, and, on the other, on the common interests and ties which so closely unite us to the Blessed Virgin.

We will say a few words on both, for we shall find that nothing is more capable of exciting in our hearts those lively sentiments of tender love, which have animated so many of the saints, and which are still experienced by numbers of faithful servants in the Church of God.

In speaking of beauty, we must, when the Blessed Virgin is concerned, lay aside all ideas of mortal or earthly beauty; hers is entirely celestial, angelic, and divine. It resembles the beauty of the Sacred Humanity of Jesus, which will be an everlasting source of happiness to the eyes and hearts of the blessed; which will transport them with joy, and cause them to taste the ineffable sweetness of Divine Love.

The beauty of the Blessed Virgin is of a similar nature, and produces proportionate effects on the joys of the saints. The Holy Spirit describes Mary as "all fair."

All beauties indeed, corporal as well as spiritual, were united in her.

The beauty conferred by every virtue and good gift of God, all the beauties of nature and of grace, all the beauty of glory, beauty without spot or blemish, everlasting, incorruptible, immortal, most attractive and most charming; beauty, in fine, which captivates every heart and mind.

The Holy Spirit, again, says of Mary that she is "fair as the moon, chosen as the sun;"[1] giving us to understand by these comparisons the extent of that loveliness, near which all other created beauty vanishes, as the stars fade away in the light of the sun and moon.

To this incomparable beauty of the Queen of heaven is added an equal degree of sweetness.

Such perfection of sweetness, in one so attractive, most powerfully incites the heart to love; and in the Blessed Virgin it is so eminent as to be one of her most beautiful characteristics.

Never were two hearts more like to each other than those of Jesus and Mary.

The heart of Jesus was the most tender

[1] Pulchra ut luna, electa ut sol (Cant. vi. 9).

of all hearts; we can say the same to a proportionate extent of the heart of Mary; the tenderness of any other in no way approaches it.

Jesus Christ gave this command to His disciples, "Learn of Me, because I am meek and humble of heart."

If any one has ever thoroughly learned this lesson, it is the Blessed Virgin who has done so—she, the perfect disciple of her Son—she, who for thirty years had continually before her eyes this Divine model of meekness and humility.

We cannot doubt that she attained the highest perfection in the exercise of these beautiful virtues.

The Church, in her praises, attributes them to her in a special manner, calling her "Our sweetness and our life," "Mother of Mercy."[1]

In the antiphon which, during the greater part of the year, concludes the divine office, she cries, "O most clement,

[1] Dulcedo et vita nostra Mater misericordiæ.

O most pious, O most sweet Virgin Mary;"[1] and in the hymn which follows vespers in her office she again exclaims, "O Virgin of most singular beauty, surpassing all others in meekness"[2] She repeats this in the litanies of Our Lady, "Virgin most merciful; Comforter of the afflicted."[3]

These attractive qualities of meekness and of mercy belong so intimately to the Blessed Virgin, that in contemplating perfect meekness she is the most beautiful example we can take.

All her sacred person—her looks—her actions—her movements—the mysteries by which she is surrounded—her whole life—breathe nothing but meekness, benignity, and mercy. The very thought of her—her name, or any representation of her—carries this idea into the hearts of all her faithful servants. It is impossible to

---

[1] O clemens, o pia, ô dulcis Virgo Maria.
[2] Virgo singularis, inter omnes mitis.
[3] Virgo clemens; Consolatrix afflictorum.

think of her, to pronounce her holy name, or to look upon any representation of her without being moved by suchlike sentiments.

This is the everyday experience of the children of her love.

THE LOVE AND THE BENEFITS OF THE BLESSED VIRGIN.

Another motive calculated to produce ardent love on our parts, is love bestowed on us.

It is one which no well-disposed heart finds it possible to resist; above all, when such love is disinterested and bestowed by one far above us in rank. The stronger and more tender this love, the more sensibly should we love in return. Now the love of the Blessed Virgin for us is inconceivable.

Her Divine Son has loved us with an infinite love, even so far as to deliver Himself, for our salvation, to bitter torments and to the death of the Cross.

After the love of Jesus, no love has ever equalled that of Mary, who was willing to sacrifice, on our account, her only Son. As no heart ever resembled the Heart of Jesus as much as Mary's did, it follows that none ever loved us so much.

In her, this love is not sterile or unfruitful; she procures for us an infinity of blessings, and she it is who dispenses all the graces we receive.

St. Bernard asserts that every grace passes through her hands.

"Such is His will," says this holy doctor, "who has given us, through her, the richest treasure of all—Jesus Christ Himself; and through her He designs to communicate to us His other gifts, which are only the consequences of this, the first and highest of all."

In all her prayers to Mary, the Church in a marked manner confirms this sentiment, so common amongst doctors and interpreters.

A little attention shows that she regards

her as presenting all our prayers to her Son, and as obtaining, of His mercy, pardon for our sins, and all the most important graces—final perseverance, a happy death, and an eternity of bliss in the world to come.

On the Ties which Unite us to the Blessed Virgin.

Let us now say a few words on the ties by which we are bound to the Blessed Virgin.

Never did any exist, stronger, closer, or more tender.

Mary is our Mother, our Mistress, our Queen, our Benefactor, our Advocate, our Mediator, our Refuge, our Hope, and our Life.

Where else can we point to so many titles applying to one person, and all so productive of the deepest and most lively affection?

With regard, furthermore, to all these

ties and links connecting us with Mary, there is no doubt whatsoever.

The Blessed Virgin is our Mother; she became so at the express desire of her Son. St. John represented us at the foot of the Cross, at the time when our Dear Lord gave utterance to these consoling words, "Son, behold thy mother;" and when He further said to Mary, "Mother, behold thy son."

At this tremendous moment, our Adorable Saviour gave all the children of the Church to the Blessed Virgin, to become her children, and she, in the person of St. John, adopted them with all her heart.

Again, Jesus Christ having adopted us as His brethren, we also became by this adoption the children of His own Mother. This position of mother, given to Mary by our Saviour, cannot be a vain and empty one.

In the Blessed Virgin herself, it excites all the sentiments and dispositions of a true and undoubted mother—love, tenderness, and all the care and attention displayed by a good mother to obtain for her children whatever they require.

We can therefore count on finding in Mary's heart every maternal disposition.

How can any heart resist such a multitude of attractions? What love and devotion does not such a mother deserve from us!

To this quality of Mother must be added those of Benefactor, Advocate, Mediator, Refuge, and Hope; qualities so well recognised by the Church, and so thoroughly understood by all her children, that it is unnecessary to pause in order to explain them further.

If to all these were united the endearing qualities of beauty, clemency, &c., what heart, however hard, could remain unsoftened by their influence, and would not rather confess that such an assemblage of perfections cannot fail to produce in return the most tender and affectionate love?

Souls who, by the light of Divine Truth,

are able to perceive all this, love the Blessed Virgin with inexpressible fervour and devotion; no child so loves its mother; no servant has such zeal for the best of mistresses, or is more earnestly desirous of her advancement.

This thought animated St. Bernard, who says, "Nothing gives me such joy as sounding the praises of Mary."[1]

He found that the very name of Mary sufficed to inflame his heart: "Thy very name kindles in my heart the fire of love; thou canst not enter into my thoughts without my experiencing a flood of consolation."[2]

St. Bonaventure experienced the same tenderness of love, the fervour and affection of which shows itself in every page of his writings wherever he speaks of the

[1] Nihil est quod me magis delectet quam de gloria Virginis Mariæ habere sermonem. (St. Bern. Serm., de Assumpt.)
[2] Tu nec nominari potes quin accendas; tu nunquam sine dulcedine memoriæ portas ingrederis. (Ibid.)

Blessed Virgin, but more particularly in the Psalter composed by him in her honour.

In this he has collected, on the one hand, all the grandest and most sublime ideas, which can be either uttered or imagined with regard to the Blessed Virgin; and, on the other, everything which the most ardent love is capable of inspiring.

Nothing, however, can equal the fervour of the love which pours from the heart of St. Bernard of Sienna when he expresses himself on the subject of Mary.

Let us listen to his words, they are worthy of our admiration.

"God is my witness," he cries in his holy transports—"God is my witness, that when, freed sometimes by the grace of heaven from the distractions of exterior things, I am able to indulge, were it only for one hour, in meditation on the glories of Mary, I am filled with such sweet consolation, immersed in such floods of delight, that, spurning from my feet all the vanities of the world, I should desire nothing more earnestly than, if permitted so to do, to fly straight to God whilst in this state of tender transport, and before the care of temporal things could return once more to tear me away from such happiness, to turn my sighs of bliss into sobs of pain, and my songs of joy into tears and lamentations."

What, then, must be the joy and happiness and glory of beholding Mary in the Heavenly City, and of contemplating her in the full blaze of her glory, surrounded by choirs of angels, and seated on a throne which corresponds with her surpassing dignity!

What joy must there be in heaven, since, even in this vale of tears and in the midst of this wretched pilgrimage, the very thought of her name is capable of giving such sweet consolation, and of affording such unclouded delight!

This is how the greatest saints have ever thought and spoken; all those who went before or came after them have been moved by the same sentiments—St. Dominic, St. Francis of Assisi, St. Francis of Sales, St. Francis Xavier, St. Theresa, St. Mary Magdalen of Pazzi, St. Catherine of Sienna, and, in a word, all the saints of every age.

CHAPTER VII.

CONCLUSION.

We will bring these considerations to a conclusion by a few words on one of the most solemn, glorious, and authentic tributes ever paid to the dignity of Mary; and, on that account, most calculated to confirm and increase our devotion to her.

I allude to the famous Council of Ephesus (about the year 431), which will ever be celebrated in the sacred annals of the Church.

About the year 428 the impious Nestorius, then Patriarch of Constantinople, uttered his denial of the Divinity of Jesus Christ and, consequently, of the Divine Maternity of Mary.

Alarmed by such impiety, the fathers of the Church assembled in large numbers at Ephesus, where, at the opening of the council, St. Cyril, the Patriarch of Jerusalem, pronounced the following discourse, the eloquence of which filled all its members with admiration, will always remain a source of consolation to the faithful, and was received with such enthusiasm that it was considered worthy to be inscribed amongst the acts of this celebrated council.

It commences as follows, and nothing grander is to be found in the works of all the fathers through the centuries which ensued:—

Sanctorum cœtum, qui a sancta et Deipara semperque Virgine Maria invitati prompto animo huc confluxerunt, lætum erectumque conspicio. Quare licet multa premerer mæstitia, attamen hic sanctorum patrum conspectus lætitiam mihi præbuit. Nunc dulce illud hymnographi Davidis verbum apud nos impletum est: Ecce jam quid bonum aut quid jucundum, nisi habitare fratres in unum? Salve itaque a nobis, sancta mystica Trinitas, quæ nos	It fills me with joy to look upon the many holy men who, at the invitation of the Virgin Mary, the holy Mother of God, have thus readily assembled here. The sight of so many holy fathers has caused the sadness which oppressed my heart to be succeeded by a sense of consolation. Now, indeed, is the joyful oracle of David fulfilled in our midst: "What can be better or more desirable than that brethren should dwell together in one mind?" We

omnes in hanc Mariæ Deiparæ Ecclesiam convocasti. Salve a nobis, Deipara Maria, venerandus totius orbis thesaurus, lampas inextinguibilis, corona Virginitatis, sceptrum rectæ doctrinæ, templum indissolubile, locus ejus qui loco capi non potest, Mater et Virgo, per quam is benedictus in sanctis Evangeliis nominatur, qui venit in nomine Domini.

Salve quæ immensum incomprehensumque in sancto virgineo utero comprehendisti : per quam Sancta Trinitas glorificatur et adoratur; per quam pretiosa crux celebratur, et in universo orbe adoratur; per quam cœlum exultat; per quam angeli et archangeli lætantur ; per quam dæmones fugantur; per quam tentator diabolus cœlo decidit ; per quam prolapsa creatura in cœlum assumitur; per quam universa creatura idolorum vesania detenta, ad veritatis agnitionem pervenit; per .quam sanctum baptisma obtingit credentibus; per quam exultationis oleum infunditur; per quam toto terrarum orbe fundatæ sunt ecclesiæ; per quam gentes adducuntur ad pœnitentiam. Quid plura dicam? Per quam unigenitus Dei Filius iis qui in tenebris et umbra mortis sedebant lux resplenduit ; per quam Prophetæ pronuntiarunt ; per quam apostoli salutem gentibus prædicaverunt; per quam mortui exsuscitantur ; per

give Thee, then, all hail! most holy and mysterious Trinity, who hast been pleased to call us here together in the Church of Mary, the Mother of God. All hail to thee ! Mary, Mother of God, most precious treasure of the whole wide world, lamp inextinguishable, crown of virginity, sceptre of true doctrine, imperishable temple, His dwelling-place whom no dwelling can contain, Mother at once and Virgin, by whom He is called Blessed in the holy Gospels that cometh in the name of the Lord. All hail to thee, who in thy holy and virginal womb didst bear immensity itself, and that which is incomprehensible to men; by whom the Holy Trinity is adored and glorified, by whom the precious Cross is adored and celebrated throughout the world, by whom heaven is enchanted, by whom the angels and archangels are rejoiced, by whom the devils are put to flight, by whom that tempter the devil was hurled from heaven, by whom all creation sunk in idolatry is brought once more to the knowledge of the truth, by whom fallen man is again raised to Paradise, by whom holy baptism is vouchsafed to all believers, by whom the oil of gladness is poured forth, by whom churches are established in every corner of the world, by whom the nations are brought to do

quam reges regnant; et quis hominum laudabilissimam Mariam pro dignitate laudare queat?

penance. What more can I say? By whom the only Son of God giveth light to them that sit in darkness, and in the shadow of death, by whom the prophets have spoken, by whom the apostles have preached salvation to the world, by whom the dead are raised to life again, by whom kings reign! Who can give utterance to the praises of which Mary is worthy?

Reflection.

When St. Cyril spoke in these words about the Blessed Virgin, before the universal council, composed of more than 360 bishops, he employed no language that was strange or new to these illustrious fathers, or to which they could in any way object.

He spoke according to the tradition of his Church, and of the churches of all who listened to him.

We can therefore assert that the praises he bestowed on the Blessed Virgin were in accordance with the language of the Church in that century, and in those which had preceded it, by the traditions of which, St. Cyril regulated his discourse.

The effect of this holy council was, to increase devotion to Mary, in a wonderful manner, throughout the Christian world.

The holy bishops who assisted thereat, spread themselves abroad over the globe, carrying with them the sentiments of devotion to Mary which they had there espoused.

Her name became celebrated in all languages, and was engraven more deeply than before in every heart.

To the testimony of St. Cyril we will add that of others, as it will both edify and console us to perceive at a glance the sentiments of many holy fathers and doctors of various centuries since the Church was established, and to learn what has been the tradition of every age, with regard to devotion to the Mother of God.

Extracts from the writings of holy Fathers and Doctors of the Church at different periods.

ST. IRENÆUS.

Ut Evæ Virgo Maria fieret advocata, et quemadmodum adstrictum est genus hu-	As the Virgin Mary became the advocate of Eve, and as the entire human race was

manum per Virginem, solvitur per Virginem. Quod alligavit Virgo Eva per incredulitatem, hoc Virgo Maria solvit per fidem.—*Lib. iii. c. iii.; Lib. v. c. xix.*

led into captivity by the one, and rendered free by the other, whatsoever was bound by the incredulity of Eve was afterwards loosed by Mary's faith.

TERTULLIAN.

In Evam irrepserat verbum ædificatorium mortis; in Virginem introducendum erat Verbum exstructorium vitæ, ut quod per ejusmodi sexum abierat in perditionem, per eumdem sexum redigeretur in salutem. Crediderat Eva serpenti; credidit Maria Gabrieli; quod illa credendo deliquit, hæc credendo delevit.— *Lib. de Carne, x. c. xvii.*

On account of Eve was pronounced sentence of death; from Mary sprung the Word, the source of life; what was, by means of one of her sex, a cause of perdition, was converted, by another of the same, into a means of salvation. Eve believed the serpent, Mary trusted the words of Gabriel; what the former destroyed by believing the one, the latter restored by believing the other.

ORIGEN.

Ave! gratia plena. Origines ait se hujusmodi sermonem alias in Scriptura non legisse. Soli Mariæ hæc salutatio servabatur. Si enim scisset Maria ad alium quempiam similem factum esse sermonem nunquam quasi peregrina eam salutatio terruisset.—*Homil. vi., in Lucam.*

Hail! full of grace. Origen remarks that he could not find this form of salutation in any other part of the Scriptures. It was reserved for Mary alone. If Mary could have known that such words would ever have been addressed to another, they would not have troubled her as they did.

GREGORY OF NEOCÆSAREA.

Ave! gratia plena, fons lucis quæ illuminat omnes in ipsam credentes. Ave! gratia plena, spiritalis Solis oriens et flos vitæ immaculatus.— *Homil. de Annuntiat. Beatæ Virginis, ve alius istius Homiliæ Antiquissimus Auctor.*

Hail! full of grace, fountain of light, illuminating all who believe therein. Hail! full of grace, springing from the Sun of justice and the immaculate flower of life.

Tua sane laus, sanctissima Virgo, omnem prorsus laudem excedit; tibi omnis coelestium, terrestrium ac infernorum natura convenientem cultum ac venerationem adhibet.— *Hom. iii.*

The praise which is thy due, O most holy Virgin, exceeds all the praise which we can give; everything in heaven, on earth, and in hell owes thee suitable devotion and veneration.

ST. EPHRAIM.

O sancta Dei Genetrix, sub alis pietatis ac misericordiæ tuæ protege et custodi nos; non nobis est alia quam in te fiducia.

O holy Mother of God, shelter and protect us under thy wings of mercy and compassion; we have confidence only in thee.

Ex ulnis maternis tibi dediti sumus, Domina nostra; tu noster es portus, O Virgo intemerata!... sub tua Tutela et protectione toti sumus.— *In Serm. de S., Dei Genetricis Laudibus.*

From our earliest infancy we were dedicated to thee, Our Lady; thou, O Virgin unspotted, art the gate (by which we must enter heaven); we are entirely under thy patronage and protection.

ST. EPIPHANIUS.

A Maria Virgine vita ipsa est in mundum introducta, ut et viventem pariat et viventium sit mater. — *Hæres. lxxviii.*

By the Virgin Mary life itself was introduced into the world, so that she is not only the Mother of life, but the Mother of all who live.

Adesto mihi, O Dei Genetrix, O Mater misericordiæ, in præsenti quidem vitæ cursu, hostiles impetus a me avertens, ac in extremo vitæ articulo miseram animam meam conservans, et tenebrosos dæmoniorum aspectus repellens; in tremendo autem die judicii, ab æterna me damnatione liberans, et postremo in numero sanctorum me referens; atque inaccessæ Filii tui gloriæ hæredem me efficiens.—*Idem, Ibid.*

Be at hand to assist me, O Mother of God, O Mother of mercy, during the whole course of my life; warding off the attacks of my enemies, succouring my unhappy soul when I lie at the point of death, and shielding me from the terrible sight of the devils; at the day of judgment preserving me from eternal damnation, numbering me at last among the blessed, and establishing me an heir to the glory of thy Son.

Sancta Virgo est Sponsa Trinitatis, ac plane arcanus dispensationis thesaurus.... Gratia Sanctæ Virginis est immensa. lapsam Evam erexit, Adamum e paradiso dejectum in cœlos misit, paradisum clausum aperuit ... Per te pax cœlestis donata est mundo, per te homini facti sunt angeli, appellati sunt amici, servi, et Filii Dei; per te mors conculcatur, et spoliatur infernus; per te ceciderunt idola, et excitata est notitia cœlestis; per te cognovimus unigenitum Filium Dei quem, sanctissima Virgo peperisti.— *Idem, Ibid.*

The Blessed Virgin is the Spouse of the Holy Trinity, and the hidden treasure of dispensation.... The grace of the Blessed Virgin is without measure.... She raised up Eve who had fallen, obtained admission into heaven for Adam, who had been cast out of paradise, opening its gates which had been closed. ... By thee heavenly peace was bestowed upon the world; by thee men were changed into angels, and were called friends, servants, and sons of God; by thee death was overcome and hell robbed of its prey; by thee idols were cast down, and the heart lifted up to heavenly desires; by thee we have been brought to the knowledge of the only Son of God, whom thou, O most holy Virgin, didst bring into the world.

ST. AMBROSE.

Quid nobilius Dei Matre? Quid splendidius ea quam splendor elegit?—*Lib. ii., de Virgine.*

What can be found more noble than the Mother of God? What more splendid than her, the chosen one of splendour itself?

ST. AUGUSTINE.

Talis fuit Maria, ut una illius vita omnium sit disciplina.... Hinc sumatis licet exempla vivendi, ubi tanquam in exemplari, quid corrigere, quid effugere, quid tenere debeatis ostendunt.

Such was Mary that her life alone is the rule we ought all to follow.... Her example shows us how we ought to live, what faults we should correct, what we must avoid, and what we should always hold fast.

DEVOTION TO THE BLESSED VIRGIN. 145

Excepta Virgine Maria, de qua propter honorem Domini, cum de peccato agitur, nullam prorsus haberi volo quæstionem.—*Lib. de Nat. et Grat.*

With the exception of the Virgin Mary, concerning whom, I can, on account of the honour due to God, make no mention when there is any question of sin.

Mater membrorum Christi, quod nos sumus, quia co-operata est charitate ut fideles in Ecclesia nascerentur.—*Lib. de Sancte Virginitate.*

The Mother of all the members of Christ, as we are, for by her charity she co-operated in the birth of the faithful into the Church.

ST. JEROME.

Postquam Maria genuit nobis puerum Deum fortem; soluta maledictio est, mors per Evam, vita per Mariam. —*Ad Eustochiam, de Custod. Virginit.*

When Mary, for our sakes, gave birth to the Most High, the curse was taken away. Death came by Eve, life by Mary.

ST. PROCUL.

Ipsa Virginum gloriatio, matrum exultatio, fidelium sustentatio, Ecclesiæ diadema, rectæ fidei expressa forma, pietatis signaculum, veritatis norma, vestis virtutis, Sanctæ Trinitatis domicilium.—*Orat. vi.*

She is the glory of virgins, the joy of mothers, the support of the faithful, the diadem of the Church, the exact model of true faith, the seal of piety, the way of truth, the adornment of virtue, the temple of the Holy Trinity.

ST. CHRYSOLOGOS.

Sic Deum in sui pectoris capit hospitio, ut pacem terris, cœlis gloriam, salutem perditis, vitam mortuis, terrenis cum cœlestibus parentelam, ipsius Dei carne commercium conquirat.—*Serm.* lxiv.

Thus did she receive God as a guest in her heart, that she might obtain peace on earth, glory in heaven, salvation for those who had gone astray, life for the dead, relationship between those in heaven and on earth, and intercourse between God and His creatures.

Singulis per partes, Mariæ tota se infudit gratiæ plenitudo.—*Idem, Serm. de Annunt.*

He poured out His grace in measure upon others, but in its fullest abundance on Mary.

ST. BASIL.

Ave! gratia plena, Dei et hominis mediatrix. — *Seleuc. Orat. in Annuntiat.*

Hail! full of grace, mediator between God and man.

ST. CHRYSIPPUS.

Ave! radix omnium bonorum. — *Presbyter Hierosol., Serm. de Laud. B. Virginis.*

Hail! source of all good things.

ST. ANDREW OF JERUSALEM.

Ave! cœlum cœlo altius. — *Serm. de Salutatione Angelorum.*

Hail! heaven, higher than heaven itself.

ST. GERMANUS.

Memento servorum tuorum, cunctorum commenda preces, fidem confirma ecclesias ad unitatem coge, imperium trophæis auge, mundum pace compone, cunctos que a periculis liberans cunctis exora retributionis diem. — *Orat. de Dorm. Deipar.*

Be mindful of all thy servants, offer up their prayers, confirm them in the faith, bring the churches into unity, make thy kingdom to triumph, establish the reign of peace in the world, and, delivering them from dangers, intercede for all at the day of judgment.

Tu sola altissima Dei Genetrix super omnem terram; nos vero te, Divina Spousa, benedicimus. — *Idem, de Præsent.*

Thou only, O Mother of God, art most high above all the earth; we therefore bless thee, O Divine Spouse.

Nemo salvus nisi per te, O Deipara; nemo redemptus nisi per te, Dei Mater; nemo misericordiam consecutus nisi per te. — *Idem, Ibid.*

No one is saved but through thee, O Mother of God; no one is redeemed but by thy means; no one can find mercy but through thee.

ST. JOHN OF DAMIAS.

Usque ad regium Filii tui thronum pervenisti ... justitiæ fons, sanctitatis thesaurus, vivum cœlum, gratiæ

Thou hast ascended to the royal throne of thy Son. ... fountain of justice, treasure of holiness, heaven itself,

DEVOTION TO THE BLESSED VIRGIN. 147

abyssus, gratiæ pelagus, Christianorum spes, angelorum domina rerum omnium conditarum hera.—*Orat. i. de Beata Maria.*

abyss and ocean of grace, hope of Christians, queen of angels, and mistress of all created things.

Opportebat Dei Matrem, quæ Filii erant possidere; etenim Filius Matri res omnes conditas in servitutem addixit.—*Idem. Orat. iii.*

It was fitting that the Mother of God should possess what belonged to her Son; but He has given over to His Mother all hidden things besides.

Maria, cœlum cœlo divinius!—*Idem, de Annuntiat.*

Mary, a heaven more divine than heaven itself!

ST. PETER DAMIAN.

Omnis creatura ingemiscit ... tandem nascitur Maria, et ad nubiles annos egrediens, speciem induit speciosam quæ ipsam alliciat Deum, et Divinitatis oculos in se convertat. —*Serm. de Annuntiat.*

All creation groaned ... but at last was born Mary, appearing when the times were overcast; she was clothed with beauty which attracted God Himself, and the eyes of the Divinity were turned towards her.

Statim de thesauro Divinitatis Mariæ nomen evolvitur, et per ipsam, et in ipsa et cum ipsa totum hoc (opus redemptionis) faciendum decernitur, ut sicut sine Illo nihil factum, item sine illa nihil refectum sit.—*Idem, Serm. de Annuntiat.*

Then from the treasure of Divinity, the name of Mary was drawn forth, and through her, and in her, and by her, all this (the work of redemption) was seen to be effected, that as nothing was created but by Him, so nothing should be restored but by means of her.

Sicut aurora terminum noctis, diei principium adesse testatur, sic et Virgo noctem expulit sempiternam, et de die diem de terra suæ virginitatis exortum terris infundit. —*Idem, Serm. de Assumpt.*

As the aurora tells that night is at an end, and proclaims the approach of day, so did the Virgin chase away eternal night, and shed upon the earth the light of that day which sprung from her virginal womb.

Exultemus in nativitate Sanctæ Virginis, quæ novum mundo nuntiavit gaudium, et totius humanæ exstitit salutis exordium; exultemus, inquam, et sicut gaudere solemus in navivitate Christi, ita etiam gaudeamus in nativitate Matris Christi. Hodie nata est regina mundi, janua cœli, tabernaculum Dei, stella maris, scala cœlestis, per quam supernus rex ad ima descendit, et homo ad superna exaltatus ascendit.—*Idem, Serm. de Nativ.*

Let us exult in the nativity of the Blessed Virgin, who announced to the world a new joy, and stood forth the founder of the salvation of mankind; let us exult, I say, and as we are wont to rejoice in the birth of Christ, let us also rejoice in the nativity of the Mother of Christ. To-day is born the queen of the world, the gate of heaven, the tabernacle of God, the star of the sea, the stair which leads to heaven, by which the King of Glory descended here below, and man was lifted up to heaven.

Maria singularis terror spirituum malignorum, specialis amor spirituum beatorum.— *Idem, Serm. de Assumpt.*

Mary is the chief terror of evil spirits, and the delight, beyond measure, of the blessed in heaven.

Sublimis ista dies et splendidiori sole refulgurans, in qua Virgo ad thronum Dei Patris evehitur, et in ipsius Trinitatis sede reposita, naturam etiam angelicam sollicitat ad videndum. Tota conglomeratur angelorum frequentia ut videat Virginem sedentem a dextris Domini virtutum, in vestitu deaurato, circumdatum varietate, virtutum multiplicitate distinctam.—*Ibid.*

This is that glorious day, more resplendent than the sun, on which the Virgin is raised up to the throne of God the Father, and, close to the Blessed Trinity Itself, calls even on the angelic choirs to be witnesses of the spectacle. All the company of angels is gathered together to behold the Virgin seated on the right hand of the God of justice, clad in a vesture of gold embellished by all the virtues, and distinguished by their endless number.

ST. ANSELM.

Decens erat ut ea puritate qua major sub Deo nequit intelligi, Virgo illa niteret,

It was only fitting that the Virgin, to whose care God the Father was pleased to

DEVOTION TO THE BLESSED VIRGIN. 149

cui Deus Pater unicum Filium suum dare disponebat. — *De Concept.*

confide His only Son, should shine with a dazzling purity, surpassing all but that of God Himself.

Lingua mea mihi deficit, quia mens mea non sufficit domina mea! omnia intima mea solicita sunt, ut tuorum beneficiorum tibi gratias exsolvam; sed nec cogitare possum dignas, et pudet proferre non dignas.—*Idem, Orat.* li.

My lips, O my Queen, are not able to utter the words, for my heart is incapable of conceiving them: my inmost being is troubled with the desire to render thanks to thee for all thy favours; but thoughts that are worthy of thee come not into my mind, and I shrink from offering such as fall short of what is thy due.

Mater sancta, Mater unica, Mater immaculata, Mater pietatis et indulgentiæ, aperi sinum pietatis et suscipe mortuum in peccatis.—*Idem, Orat.* xlviii.

Holy Mother, one and only Mother, Mother immaculate, Mother of clemency and of mercy, open thy compassionate heart, and receive one, whom his sins had rendered dead.

Quæ potentior ad pacandam iram Judicis, quam tu quæ meruisti Mater esse ejusdem Redemptoris et judicis.—*Ibid.*

Who is more able to appease the wrath of the Judge, than thou who didst merit to become the Mother of this same Redeemer and Judge?

Hoc unum precor in nomine Filii tui: dona mihi misero perennem memoriam nominis tui; sit cibus dulcissimus, cibus suavissimus, animæ meæ.—*Ibid.*

This alone do I beg of thee in the name of thy Son: grant that I, a sinner, may constantly remember thy name; be thou the sweet and delicious food of my soul.

Beata es, Virgo Maria, omnium bonorum beatudine plena.—*Idem, Orat.* lvii.

Thou, O Mary, art inundated with bliss, thou art filled with all good things.

ST. BERNARD.

O admirandum et omni honore dignissimam Virginem, O fœminam super omnes fœminas venerandam, parentum reparatricem, posterorum vivificatricem.—*Hom. ii. Super Evang. Missus est.*

Prædica reverendam angelis, patriarchis, prophetis, quæ præcognitam; magnifica gratiæ inventricem, mediatricem salutis, restauratricem sæculorum! hæc mihi de illa cantat Ecclesia, et me eamdem docuit decantare.... Ego vero quod ab illa accepi, securus et teneo et trado.—*Idem, Epist.* clxxiv.

Maria profundissimam divinæ sapientiæ, ultra quam credi valeat, penetravit abyssum; ut quantum creaturæ conditio patitur, luci illa inaccessibili immersa videatur. —*Idem, Serm. de 12 Prærog. B. Mariæ.*

Ad illam sicut ad negotium sæculorum respiciunt, et qui in cœlo habitant, et qui in inferno, et qui nos præcesserunt, et nos qui sumus, et qui sequentur.... In te angeli lætitiam, justi gratiam, peccatores veniam, invenerunt in æternum. Merito et te respiciunt oculi totius creaturæ, quia in te et per te benigna manus omnipotentis quidqiud creaverat recreavit, —*Idem, Serm. de Assumpt.*

O Virgin most admirable and worthy of all honour, O woman beyond all others to be venerated, who didst repair the fault of our first parents and didst bring life to their descendants.

Pronounce her worthy of esteem, who was foretold by angels, by patriarchs and by prophets: magnify this life-bringing mediator, the restorer of all ages! In this manner does the Church speak to me, and order me to speak.... I will not fail to hold fast, and to publish abroad, the truths I have received from her.

Mary penetrated the abyss of Divine Wisdom in a manner beyond belief to such an extent, that she seems to have been plunged, as far as any creature can be, in its inaccessible light.

All those in heaven and hell, those who have gone before us, we now here, and all who will come after us, look upon her as the great work of ages.... In thee the angels find delight, the just discover new graces, and sinners continually receive pardon. With good reason do the eyes of all creation rest upon thee, for in thee and by thee does the munificent hand of the Almighty sustain and cherish all His works.

DEVOTION TO THE BLESSED VIRGIN. 151

Quanto devotionis affectu a nobis eam voluit honorari, qui totius boni plenitudinem posuit in Maria; ut proinde si quid spei in nobis est, si quid gratiæ, si quid salutis, ab ea noverimus redundare!—*Idem, Serm. de Nativ.*

With what tender devotion must He have willed that she should be honoured by us, who made Mary the repository of every good gift, so that we know that if there is any hope, or grace, or salvation for us, it is all to be traced to her!

Modicum illud quod offerre desideras, gratissimis illis Mariæ manibus offerendum tradere cura, si non vis sustinere repulsam.—*Idem, de Aquæductu.*

If you do not wish to be repulsed, take care to offer what little you have to give, through the hands of Mary—those hands so pleasing to God.

Opus est mediatore apud mediatorem istum (Jesum), nec alter utilior nobis est Maria.—*Idem, de Ver. Apocalypsis.*

We need a mediator, with Jesus, the Mediator Himself—can there be a more powerful one than Mary?

Invenisti gratiam: quantam gratiam? singularem, an generalem? Utramque sine dubio; singularem, quia sola hanc inveneris plenitudinem: generalem, quod de ipsa plenitudinem accipiant universi. —*Idem, Serm. de Annuntiat.*

Thou hast found grace: and what grace? particular or general? without doubt, both; particular, for thou alone hast received its fulness; general, for that fulness can be participated in by all.

Filioli hæc mea maxima fiducia est; hæc tota ratio spei meæ.—*Idem, Serm. de Aquæductu.*

Here, my children, is the chief source of my confidence; here is the ground of my hope.

Ad Patrem verebaris accedere: Jesum tibi dedit mediatorem: advocatum habere vis et ad ipsum, ad Mariam recurre.—*Ibid.*

You feared to approach the Father: He vouchsafed to give you Jesus as a mediator: if you desire an advocate with Him, have recourse to Mary.

Quæramus gratiam, et per Mariam quæramus, quia quod quærit, invenit, et frustrari non potest.—*Ibid.*

Let us seek grace, and seek it through Mary, for she obtains whatever she asks, neither can her wishes be denied.

Ipsa est Virginis nostræ gloria singularis, et excellens prærogativa Mariæ, quod Filium unum eumdemque cum Deo Patre meruit habere communem.—*Idem, de Annuntiat., Serm.* ii.

In this consists the singular glory and high prerogative of Mary, that she was esteemed worthy of possessing in common with God the Father, one and the same Son.

Tolle corpus hoc solare quod illuminat mundum; ubi dies? Tolle Mariam hanc maris stellam, quid nisi caligo involvens et umbræ mortis ac densissimæ tenebræ relinquuntur?—*Idem, de Aquæductu.*

Remove the sun which gives light to the world, what becomes of the day? Take away Mary, that star of the sea, and what is left but gloom, and the shadows of death and utter darkness?

Utrinque miraculum: quod Deus fæminæ obtemperet; humilitas sine exemplo! et quod Deo fæmina principetur, sublimitas sine socio.—*Idem, Serm. Super. Missus.*

Here are two miracles: that God should become subject to a woman — unexampled humility! and that a woman should possess authority over God—a dignity to which none other can be compared.

Maria omnibus sinum misericordiæ aperit, ut de plenitudine ejus accipiant universi: captivus redemptionem, æger curationem, tristis consolationem, peccator veniam, justus gratiam, angelus lætitiam, toto denique Trinitas gloriam.—*Idem, ex Verbis Apocal.*

Mary opens to all, her compassionate heart, in order that from its fulness all may receive good gifts: the captive, freedom; the sick man, a cure; those in affliction, consolation; the sinner, pardon; the just, grace; the angels, joy; the Holy Trinity Itself an accession of glory.

DEVOTION TO THE BLESSED VIRGIN. 153

L'ABBÉ GUERRIC.

Omnium Beatorum beatissima est Maria, quæ de numero omnium electorum singulariter est electa et præelecta, elegit, eam Deus in habitationem sibi. — *Abbas Guerric de Assumpt.*

Mary is most blessed amongst the Blessed, and singled out in a particular manner from the whole of the Elect; God Himself chose her for His habitation.

Maria est thronus Dei, mater est vitæ, quia dum vitam generit, omnes qui ex ea victuri sunt quodammodŏ regeneravit.—*Ibid.*

Mary is the throne of God and the mother of life, for in giving birth to life itself, she, in a certain sense, regenerated all who are saved thereby.

RICHARD DE ST. VICTOR.

Maria fuit in omni virtutum consummatione perfecta.— *De Emman. c.* xxix.

Mary was perfect, with all fulness of virtues.

Ab hora supervenientis Spiritus Sancti, ab hora subobumbrantis virtutis Altissimi, B. Virgo Maria non solum fuit in omni gratia consummata verum etiam in omni bono et dono quod acceperat confirmata. — *Idem, c.* xxx.

From the moment when the Holy Ghost descended on her, and the power of the Most High overshadowed her, the Blessed Virgin Mary was not only perfected in all graces, but was firmly established in all which she received.

ST. BONAVENTURE.

Quid nos tantilli in laudibus Mariæ referemus, cum omnium nostrum membra si in linguas verterentur, eam laudare nullus sufficere valeret.—*In Spec. Lect.* i.

How little can we do in honour of Mary, since if all our members could become tongues, we should still be unable to praise her as she deserves!

Gloriosum Mariæ privilegium est, quod quidquid

This is the glorious privilege of Mary, that, after God,

post Deum pulchrius, quidquid dulcius, quidquid jucundius in gloria est, hoc Maria, hoc in Maria, hoc per Mariam.—*Ibid., Lect.* vi.

whatever is most beautiful, or pleasing or rich in glory, is Mary herself, is contained in Mary, or comes through Mary.

O Domina! ex dignitate qua Dei Mater es, imperare potes dæmonibus, compesce dæmones ne nobis noceant, præcipe angelis ut nos custodiant.—*Ibid., Lect.* xii.

O my Mistress! by reason of thy dignity in being the Mother of God, thou hast power to command the devils: restrain them from injuring us, and give the angels charge over us.

Certe ad hoc opus (Laudes Mariæ) fateor nimiam omnino esse meam insufficientiam propter nimiam materiæ incomprehensibilitatem, propter nimiam scientiæ meæ tenuitatem, et propter nimiam personæ laudandæ laudem et laudabilitatem.—*Ibid., Lect.* i.

With regard to this work (the praises of Mary), I readily confess that I am altogether unequal to it: on account of the incomprehensibility of the matter itself, of my own want of knowledge, and on account of the excessive praise due to her, whose praises are to be sung.

Oculi omnium nostrum ad manus Mariæ debent respicere, ut per manus ejus aliquid boni accipiamus, et per manus ejus quidquid boni agimus, Domine offeramus.—*Ibid., Lect.* iii.

The eyes of each one of us ought to be directed to Mary's hands, in order that through them we may receive some gift, and that through them also we may offer to God whatever good thing we do.

Gratia Mariæ, gratia immensa. . . . Tu ergo, immensissima Maria, capacior es cœlo, quia quem cœli capere non poterant, tuo gremio contulisti. O Mater gratiæ, fac nos filios gratiæ!—*Ibid., Lect.* v.

The grace of Mary is boundless. . . . Thou, therefore, O most powerful Mary, art more vast than the heavens, for in thy womb thou didst bear Him whom the heavens cannot contain. O Mother of grace, make us to become sons of grace!

O celeberrimum nomen Mariæ! quomodo posset nomen tuum non esse celebratum quot etiam nominari non potest sine nominantis utilitate?—*Ibid., Lect.* viii.

Most glorious name of Mary! how is it possible that thy name should not be celebrated, since even to pronounce it is most advantageous?

Nulla pura creatura tantam gratiam in mundo, nulla tantam gloriam in cœlo invenit. —*Ibid.*

No other creature has been so filled with grace on earth, or so covered with glory in heaven.

Maria non solum est Mater Christi singularis, sed etiam Mater omnium fidelium universalis.—*Ibid.*

Mary is not only the Mother of Christ in particular, but also the Mother of all the faithful.

ST. THOMAS AQUINAS.

Persona gloriosissimæ Virginis in cognoscendo et diligendo omnem creaturam personarum communitatem ineffabiliter excessit. — *Opusc. de Charit.*

The most glorious Virgin immeasurably surpassed all others, both in wisdom and in divine love.

Dominus tecum. Aliter Dominus est cum Beata Virgine quam cum angelo; quia cum ea, ut Filius; cum angelo ut Dominus; unde dicitur templum Dei, sacrarium Spiritus Sancti.—*Idem, in exposit, Salut. Angel.*

"The Lord is with thee." The Lord is present with the Blessed Virgin far otherwise than as He is with an angel; with her as Son; with an angel as his Lord: wherefore is she called the temple of God, the sanctuary of the Holy Ghost.

GERSON.

Benedicta in mulieribus, quia ipsa sola maledictionem sustulit, et benedictionem portavit; januam paradisi aperuit; et ideo convenit ei

Blessed is she amongst women;—for she alone removed the curse, and brought a blessing; she opened the gate of paradise, and on her

nomen Mariæ, quæ interpretatur Stella maris, quia sicut per stellam maris navigantes diriguntur ad portum, ita Christiani per Mariam diriguntur ad gloriam. Laus Mariæ, Laus Filii.—*Serm. de Nativ.*

the name of Mary is rightly bestowed, which signifies Star of the Sea; because as mariners are guided into port by the stars, so by means of Mary are Christians brought to glory. Praise of Mary is praise also of the Son.

Pulchra ut luna, electa ut sol, terribilis ut castrorum acies ordinata. Maria fuit quasi aurora consurgens in nativitate, pulchra ut luna in conceptione, electa ut sol in glorificatione, terribilis ut castrorum acies ordinata pro defensione generis humani.—*Ibid.*

Fair as the moon, chosen as the sun, terrible as an army in battle array. Mary resembles the aurora in her nativity; she was fair as the moon in her conception; chosen as the sun as to her glory; terrible as an army in battle array for the defence of the human race.

Nos eam donabimus innocentia Abel, fide Abrahæ, constantia Josue, sapientia Salomonis; ipsa erit pulchra ut Rachel, fœcunda ut Lia, sapiens ut Rebecca, nobilis ut David; excedet Moysen in clementia, Job in patientia, &c.—*Idem, Serm. de Conceptione.*

In her we perceive the innocence of Abel, the faith of Abraham, the constancy of Joshua, the wisdom of Solomon; she was fair as Rachel, fruitful as Lia, wise as Rebecca, noble as David; she exceeded Moses in clemency, and Job in patience, &c.

O Virgo dignissima! tu es Mater misericordiæ, thesaurus gratiæ, fons pietatis, tu ipsa es verum templum in templo misericordiæ figuratum.—*Idem, Serm. de Purif.*

O Virgin most worthy, thou art the Mother of mercy, the treasure of Divine grace, the fountain of piety, thou art the true temple represented by the temple of mercy.

Ideo Domina nostra dicitur advocata nostra; mediatrix nostra, nostra imperatrix, per cujus manus Deus ordinavit dare ea quæ dat humanæ creaturæ.—*Ibid.*

Our Lady, therefore, is called our Advocate, our Mediator, and our Queen; by whom God gives whatever He chooses to bestow on the human race.

Recurrimus ad to devote, quæ plena es gratiæ, plena per excellentiam et superabundantiam; potesne repellere, tu quæ nunquam defuisti humanæ naturæ te puro corde requirenti?—*Ibid.*

To thee will we fly with confidence, who art full of grace in all excellence and superabundance. Canst *thou* reject us, who never turned away from any one that sought thee with a pure heart?

Tam divina est Maria, ut quidquid Scriptura dicit de Sapientia Divina, Ecclesia dicat de Maria.—*Idem, Serm. de Nativ. Mariæ.*

So encompassed is Mary by Divinity, that whatever Holy Scripture says concerning Divine Wisdom, that the Church may say of Mary.

ST. BERNARD.

Maria mundi Domina et Regina Ecclesiam militantem Ecclesia triumphanti reconciliavit; pacem iis qui prope, et iis qui longe annuntiavit; profecto ipsa est arcus fœderis sempiterni, positus in nubibus cœli, ut non interficiatur omnis caro.—*Serm. de Nom. Mariæ.*

Mary, the Mistress and Queen of the world, reconciled the Church militant with the Church triumphant, announced peace to all, near or far. She is the ark of the eternal covenant, placed in the clouds of heaven, in order that all flesh may be saved.

In illa Spiritus Sancti obumbratione, tantam largitatem et copiam Spiritus Sancti accepit, quantum potest creaturæ viatrix recipere non Deo unita unitate personæ.—*Idem, Serm. de Concept.*

When she was overshadowed by the Holy Ghost, she received as full and ample a share of the gifts of that Holy Spirit, as any creature not joined to God in unity of person is capable of receiving.

Perfectiones gratiarum quas Virgo suscepit, soli intellectui divino comprehensibiles extiterunt.—*Idem, Serm. de Nativ.*

Divine intelligence alone is capable of understanding the full perfections of the graces bestowed on the Blessed Virgin.

Omnis gratia quæ huic mundo communicatur, triplicem habet progressum; nam a Deo in Christum, a Christo in Virginem, a Virgine in nos ordinatissime dispensatur.—*Idem, Serm. de Annunt.*

Every grace vouchsafed to us in this world passes by three different channels in succession; it proceeds from God to Christ, from Christ to the Blessed Virgin, and by her is usually dispensed to us.

Nulla gratia venit de cœlo in terram; nisi transeat per manus Mariæ.—*Idem, Serm. de Nom. Mariæ.*

No grace reaches earth from heaven without passing through Mary's hands.

Caro Virginis, caro Christi. —*Idem. Serm. de Exult.*

The flesh of the Blessed Virgin is the flesh of Christ.

Tantum differt gloria Virginis a gloria omnium Beatorum, quantum sol a cæteris luminaribus cœli; et sicut cætera luminaria illuminantur a sole, sic tota curia cœlestis a gloriosa Virgine lætificatur et decoratur.—*Ibid.*

The glory of Mary differs as much from the glory of the rest of the Blessed, as the sun differs from the other lights in heaven; and as these others receive their light from the sun, so does the whole court of heaven receive its joy and beauty from this glorious Virgin.

Beata Virgo in ejus exaltatione plus magnificatur a Deo et in ejus humilitate plus magnificat Deum, quam omnis creatura alia simul sumpta.—*Idem, de Assumpt.*

The Blessed Virgin is more glorified by God in her exalted position, and renders Him more glory by her humility than all other creatures put together.

Sicut Filius est Sanctus Sanctorum, ita constat quod Mater quæ ipsum portavit est Sancta Sanctorum.—*Ibid.*

As the Son is the Holy of Holies, so also, it follows, must be the Mother who bore Him.

O Maria! si cœlum te vocem, altior es; si matrem

O Mary! if I call thee heaven itself, thou art even

gentium, præcedis; si formam Dei te apellem, digna existis; si domina angelorum; per omnia esse probaris. Quid igitur digne de te dicam? Maria est janua paradisi, gloria generis humani, thronus regis eterni, lucerna mundi, Regina angelorum, terror dæmonum, refugium peccatorum, speculum puritatis, fons gratiarum, arca cœlestium thesaurorum, consolatio pauperum, recreatio humilium, solatium electorum, conductrix peregrinorum, portus naufragantium, scutum pugnatorum, mater orphanorum, tutela viduarum, dulcedo contemplativorum, advocata pœnitentium, medela ægrotantium, forma justorum, spes et laus credentium, titulus catholicorum.—*Idem, de Conceptione.*

higher still; if the Mother of all the nations, thou art yet more; if I pronounce thee to be the image of God, thou art deserving of such praise; if queen of angels, thou provest to be such. What, then, can I say that may be worthy of thee? Mary is the gate of heaven, the glory of the human race, the throne of the Eternal King, the light of the world, the queen of angels, the terror of evil spirits, the mirror of purity, the fountain of all graces, the ark of all heavenly riches, the consolation of the needy, the delight of the humble, the joy of the elect, the guide of pilgrims, the harbour of those that suffer shipwreck, the shield of all who fight, the Mother of all orphans, the protection of widows, the sweetness of all who meditate, the advocate of sinners, the health of the sick, the model of the just, the hope and glory of believers, and the patroness of all Catholics.

O igitur fæmina ab omnibus et super omnia benedicta! tu unica Mater Dei, tu domina universi, regina mundi, tu dispensatrix omnium gratiarum, tu Ecclesia decor, tu omnium virtutum donorum, et gratiarum incomprehensibilis magnitudo; tu templum Dei, tu hortus deliciarum, tu exemplum omnium bonorum, consolatio

Wherefore, O blessed amongst women, and blessed beyond them all, thou alone art Mother of God, mistress of the universe, and queen of the world, the dispenser of all graces, the beauty of the Church, incomprehensible in the plenitude of all virtues, gifts, and graces; thou the temple of God, the garden of delights, the example of all

devotorum, totius salutis radix et ornamentum; tu porta cœli, lætitia paradisi et ultra quam dici possit, lætitia summi Dei: vere balbutiendo has laudes enuntiamus, sed supple insufficientias nostras, ut te digne laudare possimus per infinita secula. Amen.

good, the consolation of the devout, the root and ornament of all salvation, the gate of heaven, the joy of paradise, and—what higher praise can be given?—the joy of God most High; we can but feebly stammer forth these thy praises, but do thou, we beseech thee, give strength to our feebleness, that we may be able to sing them worthily throughout all eternity. Amen.

THE END.

LONDON: BURNS AND OATES.

www.ingramcontent.com/pod-product-compliance
Lightning Source LLC
Chambersburg PA
CBHW020305170426
43202CB00008B/508